New Sermon Outlines

MATTHEW
to
ACTS

NEW SERMON OUTLINES

MATTHEW to ACTS

GORDON JONES

LOIZEAUX
Neptune, New Jersey

NEW SERMON OUTLINES
Matthew to Acts

© 1996 Gordon H. Jones

Originally published by CMML Publications, 1988
as *The Alliterated Outline of the Bible.*

A Publication of Loizeaux Brothers, Inc.
*A Nonprofit Organization Devoted to the Lord's Work
and to the Spread of His Truth*

All rights reserved.
No part of this book may be reproduced or transmitted
in any form or by any means, electronic or mechanical,
including photocopying and recording,
or by any information storage and retrieval system,
without the prior written permission of the publisher,
except in the case of brief quotations
embodied in critical articles or reviews.

Library of Congress Cataloging-in-Publication Data

Jones, Gordon (Gordon H.)
[Alliterated outline of the Bible. Selections]
New sermon outlines of the New Testament / by Gordon Jones.
Originally published as part of: The alliterated outline of the Bible.
CMML Publications, 1988.
Contents: [v. 1] Matthew to Acts—[v. 2] Romans to Revelation.
ISBN 0-87213-452-0 (pbk.: v. 1: alk. paper).—
ISBN 0-87213-453-9 (pbk.: v. 2: alk. paper)
1. Bible N.T.—Outlines, syllabi, etc. I. Title.
BS2525.J6625 1996
225'.02'02—dc20 96-1096

Printed in the United States of America

10 9 8 7 6 5 4 3 2 1

Contents

Matthew	9
Mark	22
Luke	36
John	58
Acts	77

Preface

—◆—

It was the puritan Thomas Goodwin who said: "The Holy Spirit had great aims in writing Holy Scripture." This we may discover for ourselves in the study of the Word of God for which there is no substitute. If the following outlines encourage the reader to do this, the purpose will have been achieved. The notes that precede the outlines of each book have been gleaned through the years and may prove to be of help, especially to young believers.

I am sincerely grateful to my friend and colleague Mr. Alan Chambers for his painstaking perusal and detailed editing of the entire manuscript, without which these outlines would probably never have been published.

May the gracious Holy Spirit of God give illumination, direction, and power in service as a result of attention to our Lord's command: "Search the Scriptures."

GORDON H. JONES

Matthew

Notes

1. The name *Matthew* means "gift of God".
2. Matthew was probably well to do and would know what it would cost him to follow the call of Christ.
3. He does not draw attention to himself but merely calls himself the publican (10:3).
4. Matthew presents Christ as the King-Messiah and speaks of Him above all else—the symbol being a lion (Ezekiel 1:10).
5. He writes for the Jews in the promised land.
6. He makes about sixty-five references to the Old Testament.
7. It would appear that the key thought in this Gospel is "that it might be fulfilled" (Matthew 1:22).
8. The term "kingdom of heaven" is used thirty-three times and only in this Gospel of Matthew.
9. The church and the consummation of the age is also mentioned only in this Gospel.
10. There are three important discourses in Matthew's Gospel
    a. The sermon on the mount (5:1-7:29)
    b. The parables of the kingdom (13:1-52)
    c. The Olivet discourse (24:1-25:46)
11. Matthew records twenty miracles and twenty-one parables.

General Outline

I. Presentation and Precepts of Christ (1:1-7:29)
II. Parables and Power of Christ (8:1-23:39)
III. Predictions and Passion of Christ (24:1-27:66)
IV. Proofs and the Promise of Christ (28:1-20)

Detailed Outline

I. PRESENTATION AND PRECEPTS OF CHRIST (1:1-7:29)
   A. Matthew 1:1-4:11
      1. Ancestry of Christ—Forty Generations Recorded (1:1-17)
      2. Announcement about Christ by the Angel (1:18-25)
         a. Circumstances and Conception Explained (1:18-20)
         b. Concern Caused Evident to Joseph (1:19)
         c. Counsel and Comfort Expressed to Joseph (1:20-23)
         d. Compliance and Contentment Experienced (1:24-25)
      3. Advent of Christ (2:1-23)
         a. Worship of Visitors Coming from Afar (2:1-12)
            (1) Star
            (2) Search
            (3) Submission
            (4) Sense
         b. Warning in the Vision Given (2:13-15)
            (1) Announcement
            (2) Accord
            (3) Arrival
         c. Willful Viciousness of Herod in Murdering Innocents (2:16)
         d. Women's Voices Heard in Lamentation (2:17-18)
         e. Willingness to Venture in Faith by Joseph (2:19-23)
      4. Associate of Christ (3:1-12)
         a. A Man Presented to the Nation—John the Baptist (3:1-4)
         b. A Mission Planned—To Preach and Prepare the Way (3:1-4)
         c. A Message Proclaimed—To Repent and Prove It (3:5-12)
      5. Appearance of Christ (3:13-4:11)
         a. His Baptism in Water—Reference to Trinity (3:16-17)
         b. His Bread in the Wilderness—The Word of God (4:1-4)

  c. His Boldness in Witness—Under Temptation (4:5-11)
B. Matthew 4:12-25
 1. Commencement of His Public Ministry (4:12-17)
  a. Personal Movements of Christ—Nazareth to Capernaum (4:12-13)
  b. Prophetic Message of Isaiah Fulfilled (4:14-16)
  c. Preaching Ministry of Christ Begins (4:17)
 2. Call of Disciples to Follow (4:18-25)
  a. Forsaking All for the Lord—A New Life of Faith (4:19-21)
  b. Following the Lord—As He May Lead (4:20-22)
  c. Fame of the Lord—Spread Everywhere (4:23-25)
C. Matthew 5:1-7:29
 1. Characteristics of the Precepts (5:1-16)
  a. Humility and Meekness Brings Position and Inheritance (5:3-5)
  b. Hunger and Thirst Leads to Desired Fulfillment (5:6-7)
  c. Heart-pure and Peacemakers Receive Their Reward (5:8-9)
  d. Humiliated and Persecuted—They, Theirs; You, Yours (5:11-12)
  e. Holy and Harnessed with the Lord (5:13-16)
 2. Confirmation and Purpose of Moral Law (5:17-6:4)
  a. Moral Law and Agreement Required (5:17-20)
  b. Murder and Anger Inexcusable (5:21-16)
  c. Marriage and Adultery Commented On (5:27-32)
  d. Matters for Advice in Public Relationships (5:33-48)
  e. Motive in Alms-giving Noted (6:1-4)
 3. Concern about Prayer (6:5-18)
  a. Display a Menace in Public Prayer (6:5-6)
  b. Defeat in Many Repetitions—Avoid It (6:7-8)
  c. Design in the Model Prayer by the Lord (6:9-15)
   (1) Devotion Focused—"Our Father" (6:9)
   (2) Desire Framed—Thy Kingdom and Will (6:10)
   (3) Daily Food—He Knows Our Needs (6:11)
   (4) Daily Forgiveness—Needed by All (6:12)

                (5) Daily Fears—Temptation and Evil (6:13)
                (6) Devotion Finalized—"Thine...Forever" (6:13)
            d. Deception in Manner and Methods—Hypocrites (6:16-18)
        4. Contentment and Peace in Right Values (6:19-34)
            a. Laying Up Treasure for Time and Eternity (6:19-21)
            b. Lighting Up the Temple of One's Own Body and Life (6:22-24)
            c. Living Up in Trust and Testifying to His Faithfulness (6:25-34)
        5. Conditions Present a Problem (7:1-12)
            a. Judgement between Brother and Brother (7:1-5)
            b. Jeopardizing the Treasures of Holiness (7:6)
            c. Justice relating to Prayer, Father, and Son (7:7-10)
            d. Joy in the "Much more" of His Grace (7:11-12)
        6. Choice to Ponder (7:13-29)
            a. Width of the Gate May Attract or Repel (7:13-14)
            b. Worth of the Fruit a Tree May Produce (7:15-20)
            c. Will of a Person in Deciding His Destiny (7:21-23)
            d. Wisdom of the Builder Apparent to All (7:24-29)

II. PARABLES AND THE POWER OF CHRIST (8:1-23:39)
    A. Matthew 8:1-34
        1. Cleansing for the Leper—Worship and Willingness (8:1-4)
        2. Confession from the Centurion—Faith and Reward (8:5-13)
        3. Cures for Peter's Mother-in-law and Others (8:14-18)
        4. Counting the Cost of Discipleship (8:19-22)
        5. Control in His Hands (8:23-27)
            a. Tempest
            b. Test
            c. Triumph
        6. Casting Out Devils (8:28-34)
            a. Fears
            b. Fright
            c. Freedom
    B. Matthew 9:1-38
        1. Controversy (9:1-8)

  a. Palsied Man the Object of Their Attention (9:2,6)
  b. Power to Perform Miracles the Lord's (9:2,6)
  c. Protest of Scribes against the Lord (9:3)
  d. Praise of the Witnesses of the Miracle (9:8)
 2. Call of Matthew (9:9-13)
  a. Opportunity
  b. Objections
  c. Observations
 3. Contrasts (9:14-17)
  a. Question (9:14)
  b. Answer (9:15-17)
 4. Comforts for Five Suppliants (9:18-34)
  a. Dying Daughter in Need (9:18-19,23-26)
  b. Diseased Woman's Act of Faith (9:20-22)
  c. Disabled Blind Men Who Followed Him (9:27-31)
  d. Dumb Man Possessed with a Devil (9:32-34)
 5. Concern of the Lord (9:35-38)
  a. Cities and Villages Visited (9:35)
  b. Compassion for Condition of the People (9:36)
  c. Challenge of the Work among Them (9:37)
  d. Command to Pray—He Is Sovereign Lord (9:38)

C. Matthew 10:1-42
 1. Appointment of the Lord for Service (10:1-5)
 2. Authority of the Lord in Their Service (10:1)
 3. Aims of Their Service Stated (10:6-15)
 4. Antagonists Expected by the Way (10:16-23)
 5. Assurance Given to Them by the Lord (10:24-42)

D. Matthew 11:1-30
 1. Perplexity of John the Baptist Expressed (11:1-6)
 2. Prophecies Fulfilled (cf. Isaiah 40:3; Malachi 3:1) (11:7-15)
 3. Perversity of the Jews Evident (11:16-19)
 4. Pronouncement by Christ on Three Towns (11:20-24)
 5. Prayer of Thanksgiving of Christ to God (11:25-26)
 6. Provision of Rest Complete in Christ for All (11:17-30)

E. Matthew 12:1-50
 1. Charge against Christ on the Sabbath Question (12:1-8)
 2. Confrontation on the Question of Sabbath Healing (12:9-13)

3. Counsel Held by the Enemies of Christ (12:14)
4. Confirmation of Divine Choice—The Lord Jesus (12:15-21)
5. Criticism of Christ after a Notable Miracle (12:22-30)
6. Consideration of Great Importance Noted (12:31-37)
   a. Defamation of the Holy Spirit Warned Against (12:31-32)
   b. Decisions of the Heart Responsible for Speech (12:33-35)
   c. Destiny Harnessed to the Use of Words (12:36-37)
7. Condemnation of Unbelievers in Christ (12:38-42)
8. Conclusion on Self-reformation Noted (12:43-45)
9. Commentary on Family Relationships with Christ (12:46-50)

E. Matthew 13:1-14:14
   1. A Purpose in Parables (13:1-50)
      a. The Sower—A Variety of Results from Same Sowing (13:1-9,18-23)
      b. The Tares—A Growth of Good and Evil Together (13:24-30,36-43)
      c. The Mustard Seed—Spread of Good News (13:31-32)
      d. The Leaven—A Quiet Effectual Work (13:33-35)
      e. The Treasure—The Gospel Worth Caring About (13:44)
      f. The Pearl—A Gift of God Worth All We Have (13:45-46)
      g. The Drag Net—Mixed Company in a Visible Church (13:47-50)
   2. A Person of Perception (13:51-58)
      a. Question Understood by the Disciples (13:51-52)
      b. Query Unrewarding because of Unbelief (13:53-56)
      c. Qualifications Unacceptable to the Jews (13:57-58)
   3. A Passage in Parenthesis (14:1-14)
      a. Conscience of a Man That Troubled Him (14:1-5)
      b. Capriciousness of a Mood That Influenced Him (14:6-7)
      c. Care of a Maid That Embarrassed Him (14:8)
      d. Calculated Murder That Ensnared Him (14:9-11)

  e. Compassion for a Multitude That Contrasted with Him (14:12-14)
G. Matthew 14:15-36
  1. The Loaves and the Fishes (14:15-21)
    a. People—A Multitude of Men, Women, and Children (14:21)
    b. Place—A Desert with No Natural Resources (14:15)
    c. Predicament—A Challenge to Faith for the Disciples (14:16-17)
    d. Provision—A Sufficiency from His Hands (14:18-19)
    e. Portion—After All Had Eaten—Sufficient to Cover Disciples' Needs (14:20-21)
  2. The Lake and the Fishermen (14:22-36)
    a. Vigil in All-night Prayer by the Lord (14:22-23)
    b. Vision That Disturbed Them in the Predawn Light (14:24-26)
    c. Venture by Peter on the Water to the Lord (14:27-30)
    d. Value of Personal Contact with the Lord (14:31-32)
    e. Verdict of Convinced Disciples (14:33)
    f. Verification of His Power to Heal (14:34-36)
H. Matthew 15:1-39
  1. Futility of Substituting Truth with Tradition (5:1-11)
  2. Facts about Defilement Explained (15:12-20)
  3. Foreigner Benefited by Faith in Christ (15:21-28)
    a. Her Hope
    b. Her Humility
    c. His Help
  4. Feeble and Forlorn Objects of His Compassion (15:29-31)
  5. Food in Abundance Supplied for Them (15:32-39)
I. Matthew 16:1-28
  1. Focus All Awry—Faith, Not Signs, Needed (16:1-4)
  2. Forgetfulness That Robs from Lessons Taught (16:5-12)
  3. Faith in Peter's Confession (16:13-20)
    a. Christ

            b. Church
            c. Charge
        4. Folly of Peter's Impetuosity Exposed (16:21-23)
        5. Followers Need Faith and Fidelity in Cross Bearing (16:24-28)
    J. Matthew 17:1-27
        1. Transfiguration in Glorified Appearance (17:1-2)
        2. Talk with Moses and Elijah Understood (17:3-4)
        3. Terror of the Disciples at the Voice (17:5-6)
        4. Treatment of John the Baptist for Christ (17:7-13)
        5. Testing of the Disciples in the Valley (17:14-21)
        6. Telling of His Coming Death and Resurrection (17:22-23)
        7. Tax Money Miraculously Provided from a Fish (17:24-27)
    K. Matthew 18:1-35
        1. Humility Session with a Child in Their Midst (18:1-10)
        2. Hundred Sheep (18:11-14)
            a. Concern of the Shepherd
            b. Courage of the Shepherd
            c. Care of the Shepherd
        3. Harmonious Service in Fellowship Together (18:15-20)
        4. Heart Searching on Subject of Forgiveness (18:21-35)
            a. Inquiry (18:21-22)
            b. Illustration (18:23-34)
            c. Inevitable (18:35)
    L. Matthew 19:1-30
        1. Husband and Wife Relationship Discussed (19:1-12)
        2. Hinderers Warned regarding a Child's Worth (19:13-15)
        3. Honorable and Wealthy Reluctant to Follow (19:16-26)
        4. Heritage of Worth for Every True Follower (19:27-30)
    M. Matthew 20:1-34
        1. Householder and Hired Men (20:1-16)
            a. His to Give
            b. Theirs to Receive
        2. Heart to Heart Talk of Christ with His Disciples (20:17-19)
        3. Humility Lesson with Zebedee's Sons (20:20-28)
        4. Healing of Two Blind Men (20:29-34)

a. Call
b. Question
c. Compassion
N. Matthew 21:1-46
1. Presentation of the King (21:1-27)
   a. Seated on a Colt as Promised (cf. Zechariah 9:9) (21:1-11)
   b. Second Cleansing of the Temple (cf. John 2:13-17) (21:12-17)
   c. Sign of Cursed Fig Tree and Its Challenge (21:18-22)
   d. Silencing the Critics—No Answer Forthcoming (21:23-27)
2. Two Parables (21:28-46)
   a. Sons and Their Respective Responses and Actions (21:28-32)
   b. Safeguards in respect to the Vineyard Planted (21:33)
      (1) Hedge
      (2) Winepress
      (3) Tower
   c. Servants of the Householder (21:34-46)
      (1) Wickedness
      (2) Destruction
      (3) Lesson Deduced
O. Matthew 22:1-46
1. Responses to the Wedding Invitations (22:1-6)
2. Results (22:7-14)
   a. Calamity
   b. Called
   c. Chosen
   d. Clothed
3. Requirements of the Law (22:15-22)
   a. Approach
   b. Artfulness
   c. Answer
4. Resurrection Explained to the Sadducees (22:23-33)
5. Reply to the Pharisees about the Law (22:34-40)
6. Rejoinder by Christ Which Brought No Response (22:41-46)

P. Matthew 23:1-39
  1. Heavy Burdens Inflicted on Others (23:1-4)
  2. Hypocrisy (23:5-33)
     a. Persons
     b. Prayers
     c. Gifts
     d. Graves
  3. Hatred Inspired against True Servants (23:33-34)
  4. Harvest Inevitably to Be Reaped (23:35-39)

III. PREDICTIONS AND PASSION OF CHRIST (24:1-27:66)
  A. Matthew 24:1-51
     1. Destruction Foretold (24:1-14)
        a. Concern of the Disciples for the Future (24:1-3)
        b. Counterfeits and Warnings Given (24:4-5)
        c. Conflicts of the Age Continue and Increase (24:6-7)
        d. Confusion That Follows as a Result (24:7-8)
        e. Conduct of Hateful and Deceptive Men (24:9-12)
        f. Continuity Enjoined on Believers (24:13-14)
     2. Distresses (24:15-22)
        a. Standing in the Holy Place an Abomination (24:15)
        b. Safety in Flight for Israel (Revelation 12:14) (24:16-20)
        c. Suffering in Hitherto Unknown Quantity and Quality (24:21-22)
        d. Security Assured for the Elect (24:22)
     3. Deliverance (24:23-51)
        a. Process of the Events (24:23-31)
           (1) Spurious Claims Popular (24:23-26)
           (2) Signs in the Sky for All to See (24:27-29)
           (3) Son of Man Returns in Glory and Power (24:30-31)
        b. Parable of the Fig Tree (24:32-35)
           (1) Leaves and Lesson—Speaks of Israel (cf. Ezekiel 37) (24:32)
           (2) Likeness to the Lord's Return (24:33)
           (3) Living Generation to See These Things (24:34-35)
        c. Personalities by way of Illustration (24:36-41)
           (1) Exclusive Knowledge of God (24:36)

                (2) Experience of Noah (24:37-39)
                (3) Exercise of Men and Women (24:40-41)
            d. Preparation of the Wise-hearted (24:42-47)
                (1) Watching for His Coming (24:42)
                (2) Waiting Expectantly for His Coming (24:43-44)
                (3) Working Faithfully in View of the Foregoing (24:45-47)
            e. Penalty for Unfaithfulness (24:48-51)
                (1) Delay—No Reason for Doubt or Denial (24:48)
                (2) Drink—No Help for Perilous Times (24:49)
                (3) Danger—No Knowledge of His Return (24:50)
                (4) Desolation—No Second Chance to Amend (24:51)
B. Matthew 25:1-46
    1. Test in Standing (25:1-13)
        a. Well-being of the Prepared Virgins (25:4)
        b. Waiting of the Mixed Company Together (25:5-7)
        c. Wishfulness of the Unprepared Virgins (25:3,8)
        d. Welcome for Those Who Were Ready (25:10)
        e. Woe of the Unprepared (25:11-12)
            (1) Unknown
            (2) Unaccepted
        f. Watchfulness Incumbent on All (25:13)
    2. Test in Service (25:14-30)
        a. Absence of the Master on a Journey (25:14-15)
        b. Anticipation of the Master's Return (25:16-18)
        c. Assessment and Account of Service to the Master (25:19-30)
            (1) Reckoning of the Master with the Servants (25:19-20)
            (2) Rewards in Excess of Service (25:21-23)
            (3) Ruin of a Servant out of Touch with His Master (25:24-30)
    3. Test in Society (25:31-46)
        a. Son of Man Seated in Glory and Honor (25:31)
        b. Scene (25:32-36)
            (1) Nations
            (2) Sheep
            (3) Goats
            (4) Judgement

- c. Succorers of Israel Rewarded (25:37-40)
- d. Schemers Who Did Not Want to Know (25:41-46)

C. Matthew 26:1-75
  1. Consultation among His Enemies to Kill Him (26:1-5)
  2. Comprehension of Mary in Her Gift (cf. Mark 14:3-8) (26:6-13)
  3. Contract between Judah and the Jews (26:14-16)
  4. Celebration of the Passover Together (26:17-25)
  5. Communion of the Bread and Wine with Him (26:26-30)
     a. Symbols (26:26-27)
        (1) Bread and Wine
        (2) No More and No Less
     b. Significance of the Act Explained (26:26-28)
     c. Statement about a Future Day (26:29)
     d. Singing of a Hymn Together (26:30)
  6. Commitment of Christ to the Father's Will (26:31-46)
     a. Smiting of the Shepherd and Scattering the Sheep
     b. Fortitude in Prayer and Failure of Peter
  7. Conditions in His Hour of Extremity (26:47-75)
     a. Betrayed by Judas to His Enemies (26:47-55)
        (1) Sword
        (2) Sign
        (3) Submission
     b. Bereft of All His Friends and Followers (cf. 26:35) (26:56)
     c. Bound as though He Were a Criminal (26:37-68)
     d. Bitterness in Peter's Personal Experience (26:69-75)

D. Matthew 27:1-66
  1. Behavior of Christ without Reproach (cf. Isaiah 53:7) (27:1-2)
  2. Blight of a Guilty Conscience Too Late (27:3-10)
  3. Barabbas of Infamous Notoriety Offset against Christ (27:11-26)
  4. Burdens of All Sinners Now Dealt With (27:26-54)
     a. Crowned with Thorns and Crucified with Thieves (27:26-44)
     b. Cry to the Father and Consummation of the Law (27:45-51)

        c. Concerning Old Testament Saints and Confession of a Centurion (27:52-54)
    5. Burial of the Body of Christ (27:57-66)
        a. Tomb (27:57-60)
        b. Guards (27:62-66)

IV. PROOFS AND THE PROMISE OF CHRIST (28:1-20)
    A. Brightness of the Morning Visitor from Heaven (28:1-3)
    B. Baffled and Defeated Guards Overawed (28:4,11-15)
    C. Blessing of His Presence to the Women (28:5-10)
    D. Benediction of Christ to His Own (28:16-20)
        1. Comprehension—"They saw him" (28:16-17)
        2. Competence of Christ—"All power" (28:18)
        3. Commission of Christ—"Go ye" (28:19)
        4. Command of Christ—"Teaching all things" (28:20)
        5. Companionship of Christ—"I am with you always" (28:20)

MARK

—◆—

NOTES

1. The name *Mark* means "the grace of God".
2. Mark is mentioned eight times in the New Testament.
3. He was the nephew of Barnabas.
4. The Gospel of Mark was written to the Romans and gives God's answer to imperialism.
5. It was probably written from Rome about A.D. 60.
6. Mark explains words that would be unintelligible to non-Jews (3:37; 5:41; 7:11,34;10:46).
7. There are only three quotations from the Old Testament in this Gospel (Isaiah 40:3; 53:12, and Malachi 3:1).
8. The words "straightway" and "immediately" characterize this Gospel. *Eutheos* meaning "immediately" occurs forty-one times.
9. Mark alone tells us that Jesus was a carpenter (6:3)
10. There are four parables and eighteen miracles recorded in Mark.
11. Christ is presented as the perfect Servant—the symbol being an ox in Ezekiel 1:10.
12. Of all the talent available, God chose John Mark, who ran away from service (Acts 13:13), to write of the perfect Servant, our Lord Jesus Christ.

GENERAL OUTLINE

I. SONSHIP OF CHRIST (1:1-11)
II. SERVICE OF CHRIST (1:12-10:52)
III. SACRIFICE OF CHRIST (11:1-15:47)
IV. SEQUEL TO THE CROSS (16:1-20)

Detailed Outline

I. SONSHIP OF CHRIST (1:1-11)
   A. Witness of John Mark (1:1)
      1. Good News
      2. Grace of God
         a. By Jesus—The Savior
         b. By Christ—The Messiah or Anointed One
         c. By the Son of God—The Incarnation
   B. Witness of John the Baptist (1:2-8)
      1. Prophecy of Malachi Fulfilled (cf. Malachi 3:1) (1:2)
      2. Preparation for the Coming of Christ (1:2-3)
      3. Preaching of Repentance and Baptism (1:4-5)
      4. Person of John (1:6-8)
         a. Appearance
         b. Attestation
   C. Word from God (1:9-11)
      1. Venue and Circumstances (1:9-10)
      2. View of Heaven Opened and a Dove-Likeness (1:10)
      3. Voice of Affection and Approval (1:11)

II. SERVICE OF CHRIST (1:12-10:52)
   A. Mark 1:12-45
      1. Desert (1:12-13)
         a. Hunger Suffered for Forty Days
         b. Hatred of Satan for Christ Displayed
         c. Help and Sustenance for Christ Disclosed
      2. Declaration of His Message (1:14-15)
         a. Galilee, Place of His First Public Ministry
         b. Good News Proclaimed
            (1) Message of Salvation
            (2) Message to Repent
            (3) Message to Believe
         c. Grace of God Provided for All Who Believe
      3. Disciples—Four Now Called (1:16-20)
         a. Work—Fishermen by Trade (1:16-17)
         b. Worth—Called by Christ Himself (1:18-20)
         c. Willingness to Follow—"Straightway" (1:18)
      4. Demoniac (1:21-28)
         a. Astonishment at His Doctrine (1:21-22)

            b. Authority That Was Demonstrated (1:23-26)
            c. Amazement at His Deeds and Power (1:27-28)
        5. Diseased (1:29-34,40-45)
            a. Compassion of the Lord for All the Sick (1:32-33)
            b. Crowd Healed and Liberated from Demons (1:32-34)
            c. Cleansed Leper Witnessing to Them All (1:40-45)
        6. Devotions of Christ (1:35-39)
            a. Prayer in Private (1:35)
            b. Pressures from the People (1:36-37)
            c. Planned Preaching throughout Galilee (1:38-39)
    B. Mark 2:1-28
        1. Challenge to Faith (2:1-12)
            a. Broken Roof—Proof of Their Faith (2:5)
            b. Bad Reasoning—Proof of Their Lack of Faith (2:6-7)
            c. Blessing Received—Through Faith in Christ (2:8-12)
        2. Call to Levi (Matthew) (2:13-22)
            a. Customs Office and What It Meant to Matthew (2:13-14)
            b. Consent and Obedience Instant (2:14)
            c. Critic's Opposition to Christ Vocal (2:15-16)
            d. Conclusions Offered by the Lord (2:17-22)
                (1) Purpose of the Bridegroom's Coming (2:17)
                (2) Pleasure of the Bridegroom's Companionship (2:18-20)
                (3) Pictures of the Bridegroom's New Creation (2:21-22)
        3. Cornfield (2:23-28)
            a. Legitimate Deed by the Lord and His Disciples (2:23-24)
            b. Liberty of David Recalled by Christ (2:25-26)
            c. Lesson to Deduce regarding the Foregoing (2:27-28)
    C. Mark 3:1-35
        1. Factions in the Synagogue (3:1-6)
            a. Cause—A Withered Hand and a Sabbath Day (3:1)
            b. Challenge—Watching Him in Silence and Derision (3:2-4)

        c. Command—A Work of Healing, Success Definite (3:5)
        d. Counsel—A Work of Hate, Scheming to Destroy (3:6)
    2. Following (3:7-12)
        a. Cosmopolitan Congregation by the Lakeside (3:7-8)
        b. Crushing Crowd Seeking Help and Healing (3:9-10)
        c. Confession and Charge regarding Evil Spirits (3:11-12)
    3. Fellow-Workers (3:13-21)
        a. Called and Chosen "Whom he would" (3:13)
        b. Commissioned and Capable for the Task (3:14-19)
        c. Crowds and Constraint; Frustration and Friends (3:20-21)
    4. Forgiveness and a Warning (3:22-30)
        a. Bitterness of the Enemies of the Lord (3:22)
        b. Bogey of Beelzebub Removed (3:23-27)
        c. Blasphemy against the Holy Spirit Unforgivable (3:28-30)
    5. Family Relationship Explained in Christ (3:31-35)
D. Mark 4:1-41
    1. Sower (4:1-20)
        a. Seed—Word of God and of Life (4:1-3,14)
        b. Soil—Variation in Its Kind from Place to Place (4:5,7-8)
        c. Schemer—Activities of the Adversary (4:15)
        d. Success—Fruit Sown in Good Ground (4:8.20)
    2. Secret (4:21-25)
        a. Meaning of Light Purposefully Regulated (4:21)
        b. Manifestation of Light Positively Reveals (4:22-23)
        c. Measure of Light a Personal Responsibility (4:23)
    3. Seed Time (4:26-34)
        a. Seed in the Ground—An Act of Faith in God's Laws (4:26)
        b. Silence in Growth—An Acknowledged Mystery (4:27)
        c. Sequence in Growth—A Process (4:28)
           (1) Blade

(2) Ear
(3) Corn
d. Sickle to Gather—A Harvest Produced (4:29)
e. Sowing of Grain—A Small Seed to Begin With (4:30-31)
f. Sanctuary Given—A Rest for the Birds (4:32)
g. Sense Given—Of All the Parables by Christ (4:33-34)
4. Storm (4:35-41)
a. Movement of the Crowd after the Discourse (4:35-36)
b. Menace of Contrary Winds Affecting Many Ships (4:37-38)
c. Master of Creation Aware of Every Happening (4:39)
d. Miracle of Calm Arresting and Controlling the Elements (4:39)
e. Marvelling Companions Asked and Received a Question (4:40-41)

E. Mark 5:1-43
1. The Man (5:1-20)
a. Circumstances of His Life and Malady (5:1-3)
(1) Unclean Spirit to Torment Him
(2) Unhappy Setting in the Tombs
(3) Untamable Strength to Test
b. Cry for Help to the Lord (5:6-7)
(1) Worship
(2) Witness
c. Command of the Lord to the Evil Spirit (5:8-9)
d. Consent of the Lord to Their Request (5:10-13)
e. Contentment of the Liberated Man (5:14-16)
f. Commission of the Lord to Witness to His Own (5:17-20)
2. The Woman (5:25-34)
a. Coming to the Lord Attempted in spite of Malady (5:25-26)
b. Contact with the Lord Achieved in spite of the Crowd (5:17,31-32)
c. Confession to the Lord Accomplished in spite of the Crowd (5:33)

d. Comfort from the Lord Assured on the Ground of Faith (5:34)
    3. The Child (5:21-24,35-43)
        a. Plea Expressed by the Father on Her Behalf (5:21-24)
        b. Position Explained by a Servant to Them All (5:35)
        c. Parents Exhorted to Believe by the Lord (5:36)
        d. People Excluded from the Child's Room (5:37-40)
        e. Pleasure Experienced by the Family (5:41-43)
F. Mark 6:1-56
    1. Carpenter (6:1-6)
        a. Astonishment Unreasonable (6:1-2)
        b. Antagonism Unworthy of Him (6:2-3)
        c. Attitude Unacceptable to Him (6:4-6)
    2. Commission (6:7-13,30-31)
        a. Power Given to Serve (6:7)
        b. Provision for the Tour Explained (6:8-10)
        c. Plans Outlined Beforehand (6:11)
        d. Preaching according to Instructions (6:12-13)
        e. Pressures of Service calling for Spiritual Refreshment (6:30-31)
    3. Conduct of Herod (6:14-29)
        a. Active Conscience That Troubled Him (6:14-18)
        b. Angry Consort That Trapped Him (6:19)
        c. Awareness of Character That Tested Him (6:20)
        d. Act of a Criminal That Tormented Him (6:21-29)
    4. Crowd (6:33-44)
        a. Multitude Following an Object of Compassion (6:33-34)
        b. Manifest Fears of the Disciples (6:35-36)
        c. Multiplied Food to Supply All Their Need (6:37-41)
        d. Many Fragments Gathered in Twelve Baskets (6:43-44)
    5. Conclusion of a Busy Day (6:45-52)
        a. Communion in Prayer Alone with the Father (6:45-46)
        b. Contrary and Perverse Winds That Troubled the Disciples (6:47-48)
        c. Consternation and Perplexity of the Disciples (6:49-50)

- d. Comfort in His Presence in spite of All Else (6:50-51)
- e. Control Perfect—They Were Profoundly Moved (6:51-52)
  6. Cures (6:53-56)
     - a. People Hear Where He Is and Come to See Him (6:53-55)
     - b. Power to Heal When and Where There Was Need (6:56)
     - c. Pleasure and Happiness So Many Enjoyed
- G. Mark 7:1-37
  1. Rebuke for the Pharisees (7:1-23)
     - a. Question of Washing and Traditions (7:1-6)
     - b. Question of Worship and Truth of His Word (7:7-13)
     - c. Question of the Word versus Their Traditions (7:13)
     - d. Question of What Is Within and What Is Without (7:14-23)
  2. Reward (7:24-30)
     - a. Desire of Faith Expressed by a Foreigner (7:24-26)
     - b. Dialogue of Facts Voiced by Christ and the Woman (7:27-28)
     - c. Deliverance by Faith Enjoyed by the Daughter (7:29-30)
  3. Restoration (7:31-37)
     - a. Affliction Suffered by the Deaf and Dumb Man (7:31-32)
     - b. Act of Sovereign Will by the Lord in Every Case (7:33-34)
     - c. Attestation Spoken—"He hath done all things well" (7:35-37)
- H. Mark 8:1-38)
  1. Compassion of Christ (8:1-9)
     - a. Multitude's Problem—They Were Fainting (8:1-3)
     - b. Means Provided—They Were All Fed (8:4-7)
     - c. Miracle Performed—They Gathered the Fragments That Remained into Seven Baskets (cf. Acts 9:25)
  2. Contrariness of the Pharisees (8:10-21)
     - a. Sign from the Lord Sought by the Pharisees (8:10-12)

  b. Significance of the Sign of Leaven Not Understood (8:13-16)
  c. Seeing Signs yet Forgetting the Lessons (8:17-21)
 3. Cure for Blindness (8:22-26)
  a. Rejected Town—Bethsaida (cf. Matthew 11:21-24) (8:22-23)
  b. Received Treatment—Unique in This Case (8:23-25)
  c. Refused Testimony for an Unbelieving Population (8:26)
 4. Confession of Peter (8:27-33)
  a. Report concerning Christ among the People (8:27-28)
  b. Reply to Christ's Question by Peter (8:29)
  c. Revelation of Christ's Coming Rejection (8:30-31)
  d. Rebuke of Christ for Peter (8:32-33)
 5. Cross-Bearing Required of Disciples (8:34-38)
  a. Identification in the Venture of Faith (8:34-35)
  b. Indication of the Value of Souls in His Sight (8:36-37)
  c. Involvement in the Verdict of Christ for All (8:38)

I. Mark 9:1-50
 1. Honor for the Disciples (9:1-13)
  a. Transfiguration of Christ before Their Eyes (9:1-3)
  b. Talk with Two Glorified Living Persons (9:4)
  c. Terror Evoked by the Presence of Two They Knew (9:5-6)
  d. Testimony of the Voice from Heaven (9:7)
  e. Trust for Them to Keep till after the Resurrection (9:8-10)
  f. Teaching about Elijah and John the Baptist (9:11-13)
 2. Helplessness without Him (9:14-29)
  a. Inability of the Disciples to Help the Child (9:14-18)
  b. Capability of Christ to Meet the Need (9:19-27)
  c. Possibility of the Disciples Being Made Able (9:28-29)
 3. Hatred by His Enemies (9:31-32)
  a. Incognito—Passing through Galilee (9:30)
  b. Instruction—Lord's Death and Resurrection (9:31)

       c. Ignorance—Disciples' Lack of Understanding (9:32)
   4. Humility—A Lesson to Learn (9:33-41)
       a. Pride Revealed among the Disciples (9:33-34)
       b. Principle Recorded with a Child among Them (9:35-37)
       c. Prejudice Resolved among the Disciples (9:38-40)
       d. Promise of Reward because of Gifts in His Name (9:41)
   5. Hell—A Warning (9:42-50)
       a. Offence and Its Measure of Importance (9:42)
       b. Operation and Its Alternative (9:43-48)
       c. Obligation and Its Challenge (9:49-50)
J. Mark 10:1-52
   1. Divorce (10:1-12)
       a. Inquiry Instituted by the Pharisees (10:1-4)
       b. Ideal Intention of God Revealed (10:5-9)
       c. Insistence—Identifying the Law with Christ's Teaching (10:10-12)
   2. Displeasure of Christ (10:13-16)
       a. Rebuke of the Parents by the Disciples (10:13)
       b. Reception of the Children by the Lord (10:14-16)
       c. Requirement of the Lord—Childlike Faith (10:15)
   3. Disappointment (10:17-31)
       a. Character and Conduct of the Young Man (10:17-20)
       b. Challenge of Christ to the Young Man (10:21)
       c. Choice and Its Consequence for the Young Man (10:22)
       d. Conclusions of Christ about Trusting in Riches (10:23-26)
       e. Certainty and Consolation in Christ's Service (10:27-31)
   4. Declaration to the Disciples (cf. 9:31-32)
       a. Fear of the Unknown among the Disciples (10:32)
       b. Facts Unfolded to Them by the Lord (10:10:33-34)
       c. Failure to Understand of What He Spoke
   5. Desire Expressed (10:35-45)
       a. Ignorance Displayed by James and John (10:35-37)

>   b. Involvement Designed by the Lord for Them (10:38-39)
>   c. Indignant Disciples because of James and John (10:41)
>   d. Instruction Delivered to Disciples on Humility (10:42-25)
>   6. Determination (10:46-52)
>   a. Crowd between Blind Bartimaeus and Christ (10:46-48)
>   b. Cry of Boldness from Bartimaeus to Christ (10:47-48)
>   c. Comfort Bestowed on Bartimaeus (10:49-50)
>   d. Contact to Bless Him in His Need (10:51)
>   e. Cure to Blindness Instant on the Ground of Faith (10:52)
>
> III. SACRIFICE OF CHRIST (11:1–15:47)
>   A. Mark 11:1-33
>   1. A Colt (11:1-11)
>   a. Errand on Which the Disciples Were Sent (11:1-3)
>   b. Effect on the Animal and the People (11:4-10)
>   (1) Release of a Life That Was Restricted (11:4)
>   (2) Record of the Prophet Fulfilled (cf. Zechariah 9:9) (11:8-10)
>   (3) Rejoicing of the People Who Followed (11:9-10)
>   c. Entry of Christ on the Colt into Jerusalem (11:11)
>   2. A Curse (11:12-14,20-21)
>   a. Fig Tree a Figure of Israel Nationally (11:12-13)
>   b. Foliage When Fruit Should Have Been There (11:13)
>   c. Failure and Fruitlessness Typifying Israel (11:14,20-21)
>   3. A Cleansing (11:15-19)
>   a. Temple and Worship—Designed by God (11:15-19)
>   b. Traders and Their Work—A Misuse of God's House (11:15-19)
>   c. Teaching and His Witness regarding the Temple (11:15-19)

- 4. A Consideration about Faith (11:22-26)
  - a. Faith Indispensable in Our Relationship with God (11:22-23)
  - b. Fruit Inevitable in the Real Exercise of Faith (11:24)
  - c. Forgiveness Incumbent on Us All to Each Other (11:25-26)
- 5. A Climax in Questions (11:27-33)
  - a. Questioned Authority—His Enemies Again (11:27-28)
  - b. Queried Acknowledgment—Regarding John the Baptist (11:29-32)
  - c. Qualified Answer—In the Negative to Their Confusion (11:33)

B. Mark 12:1-44
  1. Responsibility (12:1-12)
     - a. Test of Service for the Tenants by the Absent Master (12:1)
     - b. Tokens of Service Sought by the Master (12:2)
     - c. Treatment of the Servants Inexcusable (12:3-5)
     - d. Thieves and the Son of the Master, and Inheritance (12:6-8)
     - e. Trouble and Suffering Deservedly Theirs (12:9)
     - f. Testimony of the Scriptures regarding Israel (12:10-12)
  2. Recognition (12:13-17)
     - a. Conspiracy to Catch the Lord by Guile (12:13-15)
     - b. Clue on a Coin Confounds the Conspirators (12:15-16)
     - c. Clarifying Command to Give Honor Where Due (12:17)
  3. Resurrection (12:18-27)
     - a. Sadducees and Their Unbelief Advertised (12:18)
     - b. Story and Its Unsuitability Apparent (12:19-24)
     - c. Scriptures Unerringly Answer the Question (12:25-27)
  4. Reasoning (12:28-34)
     - a. Commandments and the Scribe with a Question (12:28-31)

   b. Consent of the Scribe to the Answer Given (12:32-33)
   c. Comment about the Scribe by the Lord (12:34)
  5. Request (12:35-37)
   a. Query about David and Christ Asked (12:35)
   b. Quotation Acceptable to All the Jews (12:36)
   c. Question Answerable Only by Faith (12:37)
  6. Remarks (12:38-40)
   a. Pride of the Scribes
   b. Persons of the Scribes
   c. Places of the Scribes
   d. Prayers of the Scribes
  7. Reflections (12:41-44)
   a. Wealthy Giving of Their Abundance (12:41)
   b. Widow Giving Her All—Thus More (12:42-43)
   c. Witness of Christ Commands Our Attention (12:43-44)
C. Mark 13:1-37—The Olivet Discourse
  1. Circumstances of the Discourse overlooking Jerusalem (13:1-4)
  2. Course of the Age Disclosed to the Disciples (13:5-37)
  3. Conditions Described of Trials and Troubles (13:5-37)
  4. Coming Declared When He Returns in Glory (13:24-27)
  5. Case of the Fig Tree Defined—Israel a Nation (13:28-33)
  6. Continuity of Watchfulness Desired (13:34-37)
D. Mark 14:1-72
  1. Opponents of Christ Scheme to Take Him (14:1-2)
  2. Offering of Value Given in Bethany (14:3-9)
   a. Anointing His Head with Spikenard (14:3)
   b. Anger of Charity Workers (14:4-5)
   c. Acknowledgment of Her by Christ (14:6-9)
  3. Outcast Plots with the Enemies of Christ (14:10-11)
  4. Orders of Christ regarding the Passover (14:12-16)
   a. Pitcher
   b. Place
   c. Preparation

5. Ordinance to Remember (14:17-25)
   a. Sorrow of the Disciples—Evident and Expressed (14:17-19)
   b. Sign in the Dish—Betrayer Identified (14:20-21)
   c. Symbols Designated by the Lord at the Table (14:22-23)
   d. Significance Described—In Memory of Him (14:23-25)
6. Offence of the Cross (14:26-31)
   a. Death of Christ—Stumblingblock to Many (14:27)
   b. Desertion Crisis—Shepherdless Flock (14:27,30)
   c. Day of Comfort—Promised to All (14:28)
   d. Denials—Common to All (14:39-31)
7. Obedience of Christ (14:32-72)
   a. Prayer of Christ in Gethsemane (14:32-72)
      (1) Separation of the Three from the Others (14:32-34)
      (2) Sleepers Unaware of the Importance of the Hour (14:35-41)
      (3) Submission of Christ to the Father's Will (14:42-52)
   b. Priests (14:53-65)
      (1) Inquiry
      (2) Injustice
      (3) Insults
   c. Peter in Weakness and Trouble (14:66-72)
      (1) Significance of the Crowing
      (2) Sinfulness of His Cursing
      (3) Sorrow of His Contrite Heart

E. Mark 15:1-47
   1. Consultation (15:1-5)
      a. Activity of the Sanhedrin in the Morning (15:1)
      b. Accusations of the Sanhedrin against the Lord (15:2-3)
      c. Attitude of the Savior to Pilate and Priests (15:4-5)
   2. Choice (15:6-15)
      a. Injustice Heaped upon Him (15:6-15)
         (1) A Rebel Chosen
         (2) A Redeemer Condemned

        b. Intensity of Hatred Unfolded by Them
           (15:11,13-14)
        c. Insulting Humiliation Unleashed against Him
           (15:11-15)
     3. Crucifixion (15:16-38)
        a. Crowned as Shameless Soldiers Jest (15:16-20)
        b. Cross a Supreme Sacrifice—The Just for the
           Unjust (15:24-38)
        c. Cry as the Savior Is Judged in Our Place (15:24-38)
     4. Centurion (15:39)
        a. Stood an Unbelieving Sinner
        b. Saw an Unbelievable Sight
        c. Spoke an Undeniable Truth
     5. Conclusion (15:40-47)
        a. Boldness of Joseph of Arimathaea
        b. Body and Burial of Jesus

IV. SEQUEL TO THE CROSS (16:1-20)
    A. Risen from the Grave (16:1-6)
       1. Devotion at Sunrise by Faithful Women (16:1-2)
       2. Dismay over a Stone—Problem No Longer Existed
          (16:3-4)
       3. Direction to the Seekers by the Heavenly Messenger
          (16:5-7)
       4. Disciples and Simon Peter Told (16:7)
    B. Reappearance as a Guest (16:7-14)
       1. Disciples Unable to Adjust to Facts (16:7-9)
       2. Disciples Unaware of His Identity (16:12-13)
       3. Disciple's Unbelief at the Good News They Heard
          (16:10-11,13-14)
    C. Received Into Glory (16:15-20)
       1. Commissioned by the Lord—"Preach the Gospel"
          (16:15-16)
       2. Convinced by the Lord—He Is There (16:15-18)
       3. Conveyance of the Lord—Heavenward before Their
          Eyes (16:19)
       4. Confirmation by the Lord—Their Witness and Work
          (16:20)

LUKE

NOTES

1. This Gospel was probably written about A.D. 56-60.
2. Luke was a physician (Colossians 4:14).
3. He wrote for the Greek world and gives God's answer to Hellenism, i.e. Greek manners and customs.
4. This Gospel sets forth Christ as the perfect man and therefore perfect Savior (cf. Ezekiel 1:10).
5. Luke is mentioned three times in the New Testament
   a. Colossians 4:14
   b. 2 Timothy 4:11
   c. Philemon 24
6. Luke became a fellow traveller with Paul (Acts 16:10).
7. Note the universality of the Gospel
   a. To all people (2:10)
   b. To all flesh (3:6)
   c. To all nations (24:27)
8. There are about fifty references to prayer in this Gospel.
9. There are three parables on prayer
   a. The importunate friend (11:5-10)
   b. The persistent woman (18:1-8)
   c. The pharisee and the publican (18:9-14)
10. The word *anothen* translated "from the very first" in Luke 1:3 is translated "from above" in John 3:31 and 19:11.
11. There are twenty-one miracles and twenty-seven parables recorded in Luke's Gospel.
12. Luke, like Mark, was not one of the twelve apostles.

GENERAL OUTLINE

I. RECORD OF THE SAVIOR (1:1-3:37)
II. RESOURCES OF THE SAVIOR (4:1-21:38)
III. REJECTION OF THE SAVIOR (22:1-23:56)
IV. RESURRECTION OF THE SAVIOR (24:1-53)

Detailed Outline

I. RECORD OF THE SAVIOR (1:1-3:37)
   A. Luke 1-2
      1. Introduction (1:1-4)
         a. Declaration of Facts Believed among Them (1:1)
         b. Details from Eyewitnesses of the Facts (1:2)
         c. Design Formulating In Order of the Facts (1:3)
         d. Desire for Right Information and Instruction (1:4)
      2. Birth of John (1:5-25,57-80)
         a. Service of Zacharias in the Temple (1:5-10)
         b. Stranger on a Visit with a Message (1:11-18)
         c. Sign of Dumbness Given to Zacharias (1:18-25)
         d. Son of Old Age from the Lord (1:57-63)
         e. Sense of Speech Returned to Zacharias (1:64-79)
         f. Strength of Spiritual Life in John (1:80)
      3. Birth of Jesus Anticipated (1:26-56)
         a. Announcement of the Angel to Mary (1:26-29)
         b. Assurance of Gabriel to Mary (1:30-37)
         c. Assent of Mary to the Honor Conferred (1:38)
         d. Acknowledgment of Elizabeth to Mary (1:39-45)
         e. Answer of Mary to Elizabeth in Praise (1:46-56)
      4. Birth of Jesus Announced (2:1-38)
         a. Circumstances of His Birth—A Census Time (2:1-7)
         b. Chorus of Praise from Heavenly Beings (2:8-14)
         c. Conduct of the Shepherds (2:15-20)
         d. Circumcision of the Child Jesus (2:21-24)
         e. Contentment of Simeon and Anna Recorded (2:25-38)
      5. Boyhood of Jesus (2:39-52)
         a. Silence of the Years at Nazareth (2:39-40)
         b. Services of the Family Every Year at Jerusalem (2:41-42)
         c. Supposition of Joseph and Mary regarding Jesus (2:45-48)
         d. Sorrow and Search of Mary and Joseph for Jesus (2:45-48)
         e. Submission of Jesus to Them Both at Nazareth (2:49-52)

- B. Luke 3
    1. Baptist and His Ministry (3:1-20)
        a. Person and His Privileges As the Herald of Christ (3:1-2)
        b. Place of His Witness and Work—The Jordan Valley (3:3)
        c. Preaching of Repentance—His Reasoning and Rectitude (3:3-15)
        d. Prediction of the Coming of Christ (3:16-18)
        e. Persecution of Herod in Imprisoning the Baptist (3:19-20)
    2. Baptism of Jesus in Jordan (3:21-22)
        a. Approach to John
        b. Appearance of a Dove
        c. Approval of the Father
    3. Birthright of Jesus through David, Judah, and Abraham (3:23-38)

II. RESOURCES OF THE SAVIOR (4:1-21:38)
    A. Luke 4
        1. Satanic Temptation (4:1-3)
            a. Attacked by the Devil in the Wilderness (4:1-2)
            b. Argument and Dialogue between Christ and Satan (4:3-11)
            c. Answers to, and Defeat of the Devil by Christ (4:12-13)
            d. Ascendancy Displayed by Christ over the Evil One (4:13)
        2. Synagogue Trials (4:14-37)
            a. Acclaim of Many throughout Galilee (4:14-15)
            b. Anointed of the Lord to Preach and Heal (4:16-19)
            c. Attitude of His Neighbors Revealed (4:20-22)
            d. Attention of the People to His Remarks (4:23-27)
            e. Antagonism of the Critics against Him (4:28-30)
            f. Astonishment of the People at His Authority (4:31-37)
        3. Sicknesses Treated (4:38-44)
            a. Mother of Simon Peter's Wife Healed (4:38)
            b. Ministry She Gave Them Afterward (4:39)

    c. Multitude Who Gathered at the Door for Help (4:40-42)
    d. "Must" of Preaching to Those Beyond (4:43-44)
 B. Luke 5
  1. Catch and Its Consequence (5:1-11)
    a. Fishermen at Their Work (5:1-2)
    b. Favor Asked by the Lord (5:3)
    c. Fish Abundantly Supplied (5:4-7)
    d. Followers of Christ Forsake All (5:8-11)
  2. Cleansing of the Leper (5:12-16)
    a. Malady Fully Possessing the Sufferer (5:12)
    b. Method of Helping by Personal Touch (5:13)
    c. Mosaic Law Adhered To in Its Demands (5:14)
    d. Multitude Spread His Fame Around (5:15-16)
  3. Crowded House (5:17-26)
    a. Friends of the Sick Man to His Rescue (5:17-19)
    b. Faith of the Friends That Brought Him (5:20)
    c. Forgiveness of Sins before Bodily Healing (5:20,24)
    d. Faultfinding Pharisees There as Usual (5:21)
    e. Freedom of Movement of the Paralytic (5:23-25)
    f. Fear of the Company of Witnesses (5:26)
  4. Call of Matthew (5:27-35)
    a. Customs Office—Center of His Working Life (5:27)
    b. Compliance of Matthew to the Personal Call (5:28)
    c. Company of Publicans Entertained by Matthew (5:29)
    d. Complaints of the Pharisees at His Associations (5:30)
    e. Comparisons and Contrasts in Answer to Them (5:31-35)
  5. Comment of Christ (5:36-39)
    a. Parables about Old and New Cloth and Wine
    b. Principles Apparent in Old and New Lives
    c. Preservation Assured When Both Are New
 C. Luke 6
  1. The Sabbath (6:1-1)
    a. Corn Eaten on the Sabbath Day (6:1)
    b. Criticism Expressed by the Pharisees (6:2)

           c. Classic Example of David Quoted (6:3-5)
           d. Continued Enmity on Another Sabbath (6:6-11)
               (1) Withered Hand of a Sufferer (6:6)
               (2) Watchful Hearers in the Synagogue (6:7)
               (3) Wonderful Healer in Their Midst (6:8-10)
               (4) Wrathful Hate of Maddened Enemies (6:11)
        2. The Selection (6:12-19)
           a. Choice, after Prayer, of Twelve Disciples (6:12-16)
           b. Crowds in the Plain Attracted to Him (6:17)
           c. Contact Personal and Cure Immediate (6:18-19)
        3. The Sermon (6:20-46)
           a. Features of the Beatitudes—Blessings He Gives (6:20-23)
           b. Fidelity of Behavior—Being His Witnesses (6:24-38)
           c. Fellowship of Brethren—To Behold and Beware (6:39-42)
           d. Fruitbearing—Brought from Treasure Within (6:43-46)
        4. The Significance of the Sermon (6:46-49)
           a. Application Related to Hearing—Doing (6:46-47)
           b. Accord Reveals Safety in Right Action (6:48)
           c. Apathy and Ruin of Hearing with No Right Action (6:49)
   D. Luke 7
        1. A Faith (7:1-10)
           a. Request of a Centurion for Help from the Lord (7:1-3)
           b. Respect of the Jews for the Centurion (7:4-5)
           c. Reaction of the Centurion to the Lord's Approach (7:6-8)
           d. Remarks of Christ Commending the Centurion (7:9)
           e. Restoration of the Servant in Question (7:10)
        2. A Funeral (7:11-18)
           a. Only Son of His Mother (7:11-12)
           b. Occasion of Sorrowing Mourners (7:12)
           c. Opportunity Seized by the Master (7:13)
           d. Order by the Savior Manifesting His Power (7:14-15)
           e. Obvious Sign—Miracle to the Multitude (7:16-18)

3. A Friend (7:19-35)
   a. Servants Enquiry for John about the Lord Jesus (7:19-20)
   b. Signs Encourage the Messengers to Report to John (7:21-23)
   c. Savior Eulogizes in Testifying of John the Baptist (7:24-27)
   d. Status Explained to Hearers of John the Baptist (7:28-29)
   e. Stupidity Evident among the Religious Rulers (7:30-35)
4. A Feast (7:36-50)
   a. Loaded Conscience—She Stood Humbly behind Him (7:36-38)
   b. Little Criticism—Shown by the Host (7:39,49)
   c. Lesson Considered—Showing Her Motive (7:40-43)
   d. Lack of Courtesy—Suffered by the Lord (7:44-46)
   e. Lot of Comfort—She Had Her Sins Forgiven (7:47-50)

E. Luke 8
  1. The Savior (8:1-3)
     a. Widespread Ministry—"Every city and village" (8:1)
     b. Well-wishers—"Ministered unto him" (8:2-3)
  2. The Sower (8:4-15)
     a. Seed as the Word Presented to All (8:4-5,11)
     b. Soil as the World Presenting Variety (8:5-12)
     c. Sprouting or Withering of the Seed Dependent on the Soil (8:6-7)
     d. Success in This Work (8:15)
        (1) Hearing
        (2) Keeping
        (3) Producing
  3. The Secrets (8:16-21)
     a. Revelation by Light of Hidden Things (8:16-17)
     b. Responsibility of Hearing and Receiving (8:18)
     c. Relationship of the Lord's Family Then and Now (8:19-21)
  4. The Storm (8:22-25)
     a. Contrary Sea—Experience Did Not Help (8:22-23)

- b. Composed Sleeper—Ever Ready for Crisis (8:23-24)
- c. Command for Silence—Elements in His Control (8:24)
- d. Confession of Surprise—"What manner of man is this?" (8:25)
5. The Sufferer (8:26-39)
    - a. Condition and Loneliness of a Demented Man (8:26-27)
    - b. Cry to the Lord Who Alone Could Help (8:28)
    - c. Command of the Lord of Sufficient Life (8:29-30)
    - d. Consent Given to the Legion to Depart (8:31-33)
    - e. Conclusion of Liberty of Life to One (8:34-39)
        (1) Clothed
        (2) Contented
        (3) Commissioned
6. The Sick Matron (8:43-48)
    - a. Coming to Christ Not an Easy Task (8:43-44)
    - b. Contact with Christ Made in spite of Crowds (8:44)
    - c. Cured by Christ—A Result of Faith in Action (8:44,48)
    - d. Confession to Christ before the People (8:47)
    - e. Comfort from Christ Who Ever Rewards Faith (8:48)
7. The Sick Maid (8:40-42,49-56)
    - a. Child Past All Human Help (8:42)
    - b. Coming of a Parent Pleading for His Help (8:41-42)
    - c. Crowd Persisting in Going Along (8:42)
    - d. Challenge of Personal Faith of the Father (8:50-52)
    - e. Charge to the Parents to Say Nothing (8:56)

F. Luke 9
1. Called and Commissioned (9:1-9)
    - a. Power for the Disciples Given by the Lord (9:1)
    - b. Purpose Declared to Preach and Heal (9:2)
    - c. Plan Defined as to Practice and Provision (9:3-5)
    - d. Progress Demonstrated by Their Activities Everywhere (9:6)

                e. Perplexity and Desire of Herod about the Lord
                   (9:7-9)
            2. Crowds in the Country (9:10-17)
                a. Fellowship Report (9:10)
                b. Followers Received and Healed (9:11)
                c. Food Resources Supplied by His Hands (9:12-16)
                d. Filled and Replete—A Satisfied Crowd (9:17)
                e. Fragments Remaining Sufficient for Servers (9:17)
            3. Christ and the Cross (9:18-27)
                a. Inquiry Christ Made about Himself to the Disciples
                   (9:18-21)
                b. Information He Gave about His death and
                   Resurrection (9:22)
                c. Identity Required of Discipleship (9:23-27)
            4. Change of Countenance (9:28-36)
                a. Transfiguration Witnessed by Three Disciples
                   (9:28-29)
                b. Talk with Moses and Elijah Recognized as Such
                   (9:30-31)
                c. Trust at Hearing a Voice from a Cloud (9:32-33)
                d. Testimony of God to Christ for the Disciples
                   (9:34-36)
            5. Child is Cured (9:37-43)
                a. Son a Victim of Devil Possession (9:37-38)
                b. Spirit Vicious Ill-Treating the Boy (9:39,42)
                c. Savior Victorious over the Evil Spirit (9:42-43)
            6. Call to Consider (9:44-48)
                a. Sayings Misunderstood Even after So Much
                   Teaching (9:44-45)
                b. Self-Life Misplaced Showing Arrogance instead of
                   Humility (9:46)
                c. Significance of the Message Applied through a
                   Child (9:47-48)
            7. Challenge and Commitment (9:49-62)
                a. Sectarians (9:49-50)
                    (1) Forbidden by Us—Disciples
                    (2) Following Not Us—Disciples
                    (3) Fellowship with Us—Christ
                b. Samaritans (9:51-56)
                    (1) Movement Southwards toward Jerusalem (9:51)

- (2) Messengers Sent to Prepare the Way (9:52)
- (3) Manner of Spirit Unknown to Disciples (9:53-55)
- (4) Motive of the Savior's Mission (9:56)
  - c. Servants (9:57-62)
    - (1) Willingness to Serve—A Responsible Step Proposed (9:57)
    - (2) Way of Service—Counting the Cost Involved (9:58-61)
    - (3) Worthiness in Service—Pressing On, Not Looking Back (9:62)

G. Luke 10
  1. Appointment (10:1-12)
     a. Men Chosen—Seventy in Number to Go Two by Two (10:1)
     b. Manner of Conduct in Service Explained (10:2-8)
     c. Message Clarified—Sickness Healed and Preaching (10:9)
     d. Methods and Conduct—If a City Refuses the Servant (10:10-12)
  2. Announcement of Condemnation against Three Cities (10:13-15)
     a. Chorazin
     b. Bethsaida
     c. Capernaum
  3. Admonition (10:17-20)
     a. Service of the Seventy Reported (10:17)
     b. Satanic Spirits Overcome (10:18-19)
     c. Satisfaction and Security of Having One's Name Written in Heaven (10:20)
  4. Assurance (10:21-24)
     a. Truth Hidden from the Worldly Wise (20:21)
     b. Truth Held for Us by the Lord (10:22-23)
     c. Truth Heard Freely by the Disciples (10:24)
  5. Answers (10:25-37)
     a. Lawyer and a Leading Question Asked (10:25)
     b. Lord and the Law (10:26-28)
     c. Lesson for the Lawyer—A Good Samaritan (10:29-35)
        (1) Need of the Sufferer

                (2) Nature of the Passersby
                (3) Neighbor Who Helps
        6. Assessment (10:38-42)
            a. Sisters's Concern—Separate Ideas Expressed (10:38-39)
            b. Situation Crisis—Speaking in Haste (10:40)
            c. Selection and Care—Stating the Facts (10:41-42)
    H. Luke 11
        1. Prayer (11:1-4)
            a. Disciples Request to Be Taught How to Pray (11:1)
            b. Directions Recorded in a Model to Follow (11:2-4)
                (1) Devotion Focused on God the Father (11:2)
                    (a) Relationship, "Our Father"
                    (b) Residence, "Which art in heaven"
                    (c) Reverence, "Hallowed be thy name"
                (2) Desire Framed to Honor and Glorify God (11:2)
                    (a) Anticipation, "Thy kingdom come"
                    (b) Ability, "Thy will be done"
                    (c) Affinity, "On earth as in heaven"
                (3) Daily Food—God Knows Our Needs (11:3)
                (4) Daily Forgiveness—To Others As to Us (11:4)
                (5) Daily Fears (11:4)
                    (a) Temptations to Resist As He Leads
                    (b) Evils to Avoid As He Delivers
        2. Parables (11:5-13)
            a. Friendship under Pressure (11:5-10)
                (1) Time Unsuitable for Such a Visit (11:5)
                (2) Treatment Unceasing because of Importunity (11:8)
                (3) Triumph Undeniable (11:8-10)
            b. Father's Unique Prerogative (11:11-13)
                (1) Relationship
                (2) Request
                (3) Result
        3. Power (11:14-23)
            a. Evidence of a Miracle for All to See (11:14)
            b. Enmity of Many Adversaries against Him (11:15-16)
            c. Explanation Made by the Lord and a Question (11:17-23)

4. Personal Effort (11:24-28)
   a. Restlessness of a Wandering Spirit (11:24)
   b. Reformation of a Life by Self Effort (11:24-25)
   c. Return of the Ejected Spirit to Possess (11:24-26)
   d. Ruination of the Life in Question (11:26-28)
5. Prophet Jonah (11:29-32)
   a. Sign to the Ninevites and Its Significance (11:29)
   b. Son and the Nation—His Significance to Israel (11:30)
   c. Supremacy Noted of Christ over All (11:31-32)
6. Position Important (11:33-36)
   a. Purpose of a Candle Lighted and Positioned Aright (11:33)
   b. Plague of Contrariness—Darkness Not Light (11:34-35)
   c. Privilege of Clarity in Shining Brightly (11:36)
7. Protests (11:37-54)
   a. Invitation to Dine with a Pharisee (11:37)
   b. Intimation to Christ about Cleansing (11:38)
   c. Indignation of Christ against the Critics (11:39-54)
      (1) Bondage (11:39-44)
      (2) Burdens (11:45-46)
      (3) Buildings (11:47-49)
      (4) Blood (11:50-51)
      (5) Bitterness (11:52-54)

I. Luke 12
   1. Warning (12:1-15)
      a. Exhortation about Leaven (12:1-5)
      b. Explanation about God's Care (12:6-9)
      c. Evils of Blasphemy against the Holy Spirit (12:10)
      d. Exposure to Arrest and Persecution, Their Lot (12:11-12)
      e. Error of Covetousness, Spoken of and Illustrated (12:13-15)
   2. Wealth (12:16-34)
      a. Fruitfulness of the Earth Enjoyed by Man (12:16)
      b. Foolishness of Many Thus Blessed Illustrated (12:17-19)
      c. Finality of Death to Mankind (12:20)

                    d. Food Provided for Thought and Reflection (12:21-34)
                        (1) Consideration (12:21-30)
                        (2) Conclusion (12:31-34)
                3. Watchfulness (12:35-48)
                    a. Expectation and Anticipation of the Lord's Return (12:35-41)
                    b. Exaltation and Authority of the Lord's Return (12:42-44)
                    c. Excuses of Anguish in the Liberty of Refusal (12:45-48)
                4. Wisdom (12:49-59)
                    a. Separation of Believers from Unbelievers (12:49-53)
                    b. Signs in Beholding the Sky Correctly (12:54-56)
                    c. Sensibility before the Magistrate and Judge (12:57-59)
        J. Luke 13
                1. Lesson to Would-be Judges (13:1-5)
                    a. Record of the Past (13:1-2)
                    b. "Repent" or "Perish" Alternative (13:3-5)
                    c. Reflection, "Suppose ye...Think ye" (13:2,4)
                2. Labor on a Fig Tree (13:6-9)
                    a. Characters Involved
                        (1) A Certain Man—God
                        (2) The Vinedresser—Christ
                        (3) The Fig Tree—Israel
                    b. Case Indicated—Care of the Vineyard Israel
                    c. Conditions Illustrating the Labor Expended
                        (1) Christ's Ministry to Israel for Three Years
                        (2) Christ's Presentation to Israel
                        (3) Christ's Death—No Fruit Thereafter
                3. Liberty Given to an Infirm Woman (13:10-17)
                    a. Sabbath Devotions in the Synagogue (13:10)
                    b. Sufferer's Deformity—Incapable of Self-help (13:11)
                    c. Savior's Deliverance—Instant Healing (13:13)
                    d. Sequel—Dispute by the Indignant Ruler (13:14-16)
                    e. Satisfaction and Delight of the Worshippers (13:17)

4. Likenesses (13:18-33)
   a. Features of His Teaching—Tree, Leaven, Questions, and Answers (13:18-24)
   b. Facts about His Teaching—Testimony to Truth (13:25-30)
   c. Freedom for His Teaching—Telling It Forth (13:31-33)
5. Lament (13:34-35)
   a. Cry of Concern over Jerusalem (13:34)
   b. Condemnation of the Lord for Jerusalem (13:35)
   c. Coming of the Lord in Blessing Yet to Be (13:35)

K. Luke 14
   1. Pharisee's House (14:1-6)
      a. Question—To Heal or Not to Heal (14:1-3)
      b. Quietness—Healing and Release (14:4)
      c. Query—To Challenge Their Honesty (14:5-6)
   2. Pride and Humility (14:7-15)
      a. Choice of a Chief Place and Pharisaical Practice (14:7)
      b. Chance of Change to Advantage in Reverse (14:8-11)
      c. Concluding Considerations from the Lord (14:12-15)
   3. Provision and Hostility (14:16-24)
      a. Supper Prepared—Invitations Sent to Many (14:16-17)
      b. Scornful Persons—Individuals Refused to Come (14:18-20)
      c. Search Proclaimed—Invitations to Any and Everyone (14:18-20)
      d. Satisfaction and Pleasure in spite of Defaulters (14:21-24)
   4. Proof of Our Honesty (14:25-35)
      a. Total Commitment—In Fidelity and Fellowship (14:25-27)
      b. Tower and the Costs—Stocktaking Involved (14:28-30)
      c. Test of Capabilities—Taking Counsel Together (14:31-32)
      d. Taste and Condition—Salt and Its Savor (14:33-35)

L. Luke 15
   1. The Lost Sheep (15:1-7)
      a. Congregations's Secret Desire (15:1-2)
      b. Cause of the Search Disclosed (15:3-4)
      c. Character of the Shepherd Displayed (15:4)
      d. Conclusion of the Search Declared (15:6-7)
   2. The Lost Silver (15:8-10)
      a. Piece of Silver and Its Significance (15:8)
      b. Persistent Search and Satisfaction (15:8-9)
      c. Proclaimed Success and Sharing with Others (15:9-10)
   3. The Lost Son (15:11-32)
      a. Request of the Son—His Immaturity Shown (15:11-12)
      b. Ruin of the Son—His Irresponsibility Shown (15:13-16)
      c. Repentance of the Son—His Inquiry within Himself (15:17-19)
      d. Return of the Son—Indicating Faith in Action (15:20-21)
      e. Rejoicing and Satisfaction—Identity with the Father (15:22-24)
      f. Resentment and Segregation—The Indignant Brother (15:25-30)
      g. Reasoning and Sympathy—An Understanding Father (15:31-32)
M. Luke 16
   1. Conduct (16:1-13)
      a. Steward's Insecurity—Faced Dismissal (16:1-2)
      b. Scheme Invented—Faced the Future (16:3-7)
      c. Sequel to the Intrigue—Found Condemnation (16:8)
      d. Servant and His Intentions—Commented on by Christ (16:9-13)
   2. Covetousness (16:14-18)
      a. Derision of the Pharisees against the Lord (16:14)
      b. Declaration of the Prophets and Preaching (16:15-17)
      c. Divorce Position Explained by the Lord (16:18)
   3. Choice (16:19-31)
      a. Contrast in Life and in Death (16:19-23)

- b. Consciousness in Each Case Disclosed (16:23-25)
    - (1) They Could Both Hear
    - (2) They Could Both See
    - (3) They Could Both Feel
    - (4) They Could Both Speak
    - (5) They Could Both Remember
- c. Chasm Isolating the One from the Other (16:25-26)
- d. Concern yet Unable to Help (16:27-28)
- e. Conclusion—We Must Believe His Word (16:29-31)

N. Luke 17
  1. Sin and Forgiveness (17:1-6)
     a. Instruction on Forgiveness Given to Disciples (17:1-3)
     b. Insistence on Forgiveness by the Lord (17:4)
     c. Increase of Faith Sought by Disciples (17:5-6)
  2. Service and Fitness (17:7-10)
     a. Toil of the Servant for His Master (17:7)
     b. Test of the Servant in Further Service (17:8-9)
     c. Truth in Service for All to Learn (17:10)
  3. Samaritan and Faith (17:11-19)
     a. Ten Lepers Facing an Opportunity in Christ (17:11-13)
     b. Trial of Faith in Obedience in Action (17:14)
     c. Thanks from Only One in Assurance of Faith (17:15-19)
  4. Signs and Facts (17:20-37)
     a. Within, Not Without, Is Spiritual Life to Be Found (17:20-21)
     b. Wishes and Wonders in regard to His Coming Again (17:22-25)
     c. Works and Woes "As it was...so shall it be" (17:26-30)
     d. Witnessing and Warning of a Coming Day (17:31-36)
        (1) Two Men at Night Time
        (2) Two Women in the Afternoon or Evening
        (3) Two Men in the Morning

O. Luke 18
  1. Teaching on Prayer (18:1-14)
     a. The Widow (18:1-8)

- (1) Unbelieving Judge—No Fear of God or Man (18:2)
- (2) Untiring Effort of an Unsupported Widow (18:5)
- (3) Unworthy Motive—"Lest she weary me" (18:5)
- (4) Undisputable Fact—Object Achieved (18:5)
- (5) Undeniable Truth—God Will Avenge His Own (18:7-8)
    - b. The Men (18:9-14)
        - (1) Self Complacency, "I am not as other men" (18:9-11)
        - (2) Service Complete, "I fast...I give" (18:12)
        - (3) Sinner Convicted, "God be merciful to me" (18:13)
        - (4) Savior's Comment, "This man went...justified" (18:14)
2. Touch of the Savior's Hand (18:15-17)
    - a. Rebuke of the Disciples to the Children's Parents (18:15)
    - b. Reception of the Children by the Lord (18:16)
    - c. Requirements for Entry into the Kingdom of God (18:17)
3. Test (18:18-30)
    - a. Concern of the Rich Ruler about Eternal Life (18:18)
    - b. Conditions Required by Law, and Acknowledged (18:19-20)
    - c. Conduct Right in His Life as Confessed (18:21)
    - d. Challenge to Relinquish His Trust in Wealth (18:22)
    - e. Choice Regrettable But Was It Final? (18:23)
    - f. Comment Recorded by the Lord for All (18:24-25)
    - g. Comfort and Reassurance to the Disciples (18:26-30)
4. Talk (18:31-34)
    - a. Remembering the Aim in View at Jerusalem (18:31)
    - b. Referring to Afflictions to Come at Jerusalem (18:32-33)
    - c. Rising Again from the Dead Mentioned (18:33-34)

52 ♦ Luke

- 5. Transformation (18:35-43)
    - a. Isolated Blind Man Segregated from a Normal Life (18:35)
    - b. Interest of the Blind Man in a Passing Opportunity (18:36-37)
    - c. Involvement of a Personal Cry of Faith to Christ (18:38-39)
    - d. Invitation to Ask of the Lord As He Desired (18:40-41)
    - e. Instant Blessing Received in Answer to Faith (18:41-43)
- P. Luke 19
    - 1. Publican (19:1-10)
        - a. Desire of Zaccheus to See the Lord (19:1-3)
        - b. Determination of Zaccheus to See the Lord (19:4)
        - c. Decision of Zaccheus to Entertain the Lord (19:5-7)
        - d. Declaration of Zaccheus to the Lord (19:9)
        - e. Design of the Lord's Coming Shown—To Seek and to Save (19:10)
    - 2. Pounds (19:11-27)
        - a. Purpose to Receive a Kingdom (19:11-12)
        - b. Privilege to Respond to Kindness (19:13-14)
        - c. Power of the Returning King (19:15)
        - d. Proof in Reproducing Kind from Capital (19:16-19)
        - e. Pound Returned as Kept Unproductive (19:20-26)
        - f. Perverseness and Retribution of the King's Enemies (19:27)
    - 3. Presentation of the King-Savior (19:28-40)
        - a. Ascent, and Commission to the Disciples (19:28-30)
        - b. Animal under His Control—In His Service (19:31-35)
        - c. Acclaim of the Crowds on the Way to the City (19:36-38)
        - d. Answer to the Complaints of the Pharisees (19:39-40)
    - 4. Prophecy (19:41-44)
        - a. Pity Expressed by the Lord for Jerusalem (19:41-42)

- b. Perils from Enemies in a Coming Day for Jerusalem (19:43-44)
- c. Payment to Be Exacted for Israel's Unbelief (19:44)
5. Purification (19:45-48)
    - a. Thieves in the Temple under the Name of Traders (19:45-46)
    - b. Teaching in the Temple Undeniable Truth from God (19:47)
    - c. Treachery in the Temple from Unprincipled Teachers (19:47-48)

Q. Luke 20
1. Preaching and Priests (20:1-8)
    - a. Attack on His Authority from the Adversaries (20:1-2)
    - b. Altercation of Opinions and the Answer Offered (20:3-8)
2. Parable and Portent (20:9-19)
    - a. Vineyard: A Picture of the Land of Israel (20:9)
    - b. Vinedressers: The People of Israel in the Land (20:9)
    - c. Visiting Servants: The Prophets to Israel (20:10-15)
    - d. Violence Practiced against the Visitors (20:10-12,14-15)
    - e. Vengeance Precipitated by Their Evil Deeds (20:16)
    - f. Verdict Passed by the Lord upon Them (20:16-18)
    - g. Venom of the Priests Evident against Him (20:19)
3. Penny and Perception (20:20-26)
    - a. Deceit of the Priests in Their Approach to Christ (20:20-21)
    - b. Discernment of a Purpose in the Question Asked (20:22-23)
    - c. Deference to Be Paid to the Powers That Be (20:24-25)
    - d. Defeat of the Priests in Their Objective (20:26)
4. Problem and Proof (20:27-38)
    - a. Requirement of the Law in regard to Marital Ties (20:27-28)
    - b. Recalled Life Story of a Woman Married Seven Times (20:29-32)

- c. Request Made to the Lord regarding the Problem (20:33)
- d. Reply of the Lord Revealing Their Ignorance (20:34-38)
5. Probe and Pride (20:39-47)
    - a. Quietness of the Opponents after the Questions (20:39-40)
    - b. Query of Christ about David's Son (20:41)
    - c. Quotation from Psalm 110:1 regarding the Lord (20:42-43)
    - d. Question of Christ's Lordship and Sonship (20:44)
    - e. Questing of the Scribes for Place and Power (20:45-47)

R. Luke 21
  1. Stewardship (21:1-4)
      - a. Wealthy Gave according to Their Will (21:1)
      - b. Widow Gave All She Had Willingly (21:2-4)
      - c. Witness Given by the Lord Assessed True Values (21:3-4)
  2. Second Advent (21:5-33)
      - a. Declaration of Coming Events for the Temple (21:5-6)
      - b. Desire of the Disciples for Information (21:7)
      - c. Description of the Course of This Age (21:8-19)
      - d. Destruction of Jerusalem Foretold (21:20-24)
      - e. Distress of Mankind on Earth as the Age Closes (21:25-26)
      - f. Deliverance of the Faithful Ones Assured (21:27-28)
      - g. Discernment of the Fig Tree Signs with Others (21:29-33)
  3. Service (21:34-38)
      - a. Be Wary of the Cares and Pressures of Life (21:34-35)
      - b. Be Watchful of Events and Continue in Prayer (21:36)
      - c. Be Worthy of Standing Aright before God (21:36)
      - d. Be Willing to Hear Him in the Morning (21:37-38)

III. REJECTION OF THE SAVIOR (22:1-23:56)
   A. Luke 22
      1. Pledge (22:2-6)
         a. Intrigue of Judas with the Lord's Enemies (22:1-4)
         b. Infamy of Judas without a Just Cause (22:4-5)
         c. Intention of Judas to Betray the Lord (22:6)
      2. Passover (22:7-20)
         a. Hospitality (22:7-13)
            (1) A Home Opened for the Lord's Use
            (2) A Heart Opened to the Lord in Fellowship
            (3) Helpfulness Shown in the Furnished Room
         b. Hallowed Hour (22:14-18)
            (1) Informal—Christ and His Disciples Alone
            (2) Inspiring—Christ Their (Our) Passover
            (3) Instructive—Christ Fulfilling the Law
         c. Honor (22:19-20)
            (1) Shared Symbols with the Savior of His Death (22:19-20)
            (2) Satisfying Simplicity of the Symbols (22:19-20)
            (3) Suggestive Significance of the Symbols (22:19-20)
      3. Patience of Christ (22:21-30)
         a. Stress of Those Days Heavy on Him (22:21-27)
         b. Strife between the Disciples in spite of His Teaching (22:24)
         c. Selfishness Displayed by the Disciples (22:24)
         d. Settled Design for His Disciples Revealed (22:28-30)
      4. Prediction (22:31-38)
         a. Prayer for Peter—The Lord Knew His Weaknesses (22:31-32)
         b. Protestation of Peter—Thought He Knew Himself (22:33)
         c. Preparation of Peter—A Humiliating Experience (22:34)
         d. Provision—Past and Present Sufficient (22:35-38)
      5. Prayers (22:39-46)
         a. Attitude of Submission of Our Lord to the Father (22:42)

- b. Angel to Strengthen Him in His Times of Need (22:43)
- c. Agony of Sweat in the Crucible of Suffering (22:44)
6. Permission (22:47-71)
    - a. Submission of the Savior to Sinful Men (22:47-54)
    - b. Sifting of Self for Peter in Bitter Experience (22:54-62)
        - (1) Followed Afar Off (22:54)
        - (2) Denied the Lord (22:57)
        - (3) Went Out and Wept Bitterly (22:62)
    - c. Sanhedrin in Judgement on Their Messiah (22:63-71)

B. Luke 23
1. Condemned (23:1-26)
    - a. Denounced by the Hierarchy of Israel to the Governor (23:1-5)
    - b. Disappointment of Herod, Only a Pawn on the Stage (23:6-11)
    - c. Disowned by His Own People, a National Rejection (23:13-26)
        - (1) Menace of Perverts (cf. John 1:11) (23:13-14)
        - (2) Mockery of Principles of Justice (23:13-25)
        - (3) Murder Pilate Would Never Forget (23:24-26)
2. Crucified (23:27-49)
    - a. Company Who Witness the Deed That Day (23:27-31)
    - b. Comment of the Lord of Troubles to Come (23:28-31)
    - c. Criminals Who Suffered at the Same Time (23:32)
    - d. Cry for Mercy for Unworthy Sinners (23:33-34)
    - e. Conclusions Drawn from Those Last Hours (23:35-47)
        - (1) Death (23:35-45)
            - (a) One Died for Sin—Christ
            - (b) One Died in Sin—Unrepentant Thief
            - (c) One Died to Sin—Repentant Thief
        - (2) Dismissal by Christ of His Spirit (23:46)
        - (3) Declaration Made by the Centurion (23:47)
3. Claimed (23:50-56)
    - a. Will to Ask for the Body of Christ (23:50-52)

       b. Work of Affection by Joseph of Arimathea (23:53-54)
       c. Women Attending and Noting the Burial Place (23:55-56)

IV. RESURRECTION OF THE SAVIOR (24:1-53)
   A. Devotion at Dawn (24:1-12
      1. Readiness of the Women to Serve at Dawn (24:1-2)
      2. Revelation to the Women of an Empty Tomb (24:3)
      3. Remembrance of the Words Almost Forgotten (24:4-8)
      4. Return of the Women to Tell the Disciples (24:9-10)
      5. Reluctance of the Disciples to Believe What They Heard (24:11-12)
   B. Doubts and Discourse (24:13-27)
      1. Emmaus Road—Two Travellers on the Way Home (24:13-17)
      2. Elusive Recognition—"Their eyes were holden" (24:15-16)
      3. Events Recalled—They Were Both Troubled (24:18-24)
      4. Exposition Received—Teaching Directly from the Lord (24:25-27)
   C. Discovery and Display (24:28-43)
      1. Unique Revelation—Communion in the Home (24:28-32)
      2. Urgent Return—To Communicate the Good News (24:33-35)
      3. Undeniable Result—Confronted with Conviction (24:36-43)
   D. Design and Departure (24:44-53)
      1. Purpose of Prophetical Declarations about Christ (24:44-47)
      2. Promise and Power to Witnesses to Serve Him (24:48-49)
      3. Parting and Passing of the Lord into Heaven (24:50-51)
      4. Praises in Public—By the Disciples in Jerusalem (24:52-53)

JOHN

Notes

1. The reason for this Gospel being written, John says, is "that ye might believe" (20:31).
2. The Gospel was probably written between A.D. 90 and 100.
3. The subject is Jesus the Son of God. The symbol is the eagle (cf. Ezekiel 1:10)
4. John was the younger brother of James and the son of Zebedee.
5. After his imprisonment in Patmos it is believed he died a natural death in Asia—possibly in Ephesus.
6. There are no parables in this Gospel. Six of the eight miracles recorded herein are unique to this Gospel.
7. John records the Lord using the word "I" 134 times (cf. Matthew 29 times, Mark 17 times, Luke 33 times).—Morgan
8. The word *believe* is mentioned 98 times, the word *know* is mentioned 55 times, the word *world* is mentioned 78 times, and the word *glory (glorify)* is mentioned 42 times.
9. John does not mention the genealogy, birth, baptism, or temptation of Christ. He does not refer to scribes, lepers, publicans, or demoniacs. He also does not record any parables or the Gethsemane prayers.
10. John alone speaks of the following
    a. The new birth
    b. The Living Water
    c. The Bread of Life
    d. The Light of the world
    e. The Good Shepherd
    f. The upper room events
    g. The intercessory prayer
11. There are seven mentions of "I am"
    a. I am the Bread of Life (6:48)
    b. I am the Light of the world (8:12)
    c. I am the Door (10:7)

         d. I am the Good Shepherd (10:14)
         e. I am the Resurrection and the Life (11:25)
         f. I am the Way, the Truth, and the Life (14:6)
         g. I am the true Vine (15:1)
    12. The eight miracles in John's Gospel are
         a. Water into wine—Jesus the joy of life (2:1-12)
         b. Son healed—Jesus the health of life (4:46-54)
         c. Impotent man restored—Jesus the rest of life (5:1-9)
         d. Feeding five thousand—Jesus the bread of life (6:1-14)
         e. Walking on the sea—Jesus the succorer of life (6:19)
         f. The blind man healed—Jesus the light of life (9:1-7)
         g. Lazarus raised to life—Jesus the life (11:41-44)
         h. Draft of fish—Jesus Lord of all (21:6)

GENERAL OUTLINE

I. REVELATION OF LIGHT (1:1-51)
II. RECORD OF LOVINGKINDNESS (2:1-12:50)
III. RELATIONSHIP AND LOYALTY (13:1-17:26)
IV. REJECTION OF THE LORD (18:1-19:42)
V. RESURRECTION OF THE LORD (20:1-31)
VI. RENEWAL IN LOVE (21:1-25)

DETAILED OUTLINE

I. REVELATION OF LIGHT (1:1-51)
   A. The Word (1:1-5)
      1. Eternal Word Defined (1:1)
      2. Equality yet Distinction of Personalities (1:1-2)
      3. Explanation Detailed regarding the Word and His Work (1:3-5)
         a. Facts about Creation: He Made Everything (1:3)
         b. Feature of His Life: Light Manifested (1:4)
         c. Failure of Men to Recognize Him (1:5)
   B. The Witness (1:6-28)
      1. Persons (1:6-11)
         a. Man God Prepared to Herald the Lord (1:6-8)

  b. Manifestation of God to Man—Christ (1:9-11)
   (1) Not Reluctant to Come
   (2) Not Received When He Came
 2. Privileges (1:12-14)
  a. Receive Him—Power Given to Do So (1:12-13)
  b. Be Related to Him—Through New Birth (1:13)
  c. Recognize Him—The Only Begotten One (1:14)
 3. Proclamation (1:14-18)
  a. Greatness of Christ Recorded (1:14-15)
  b. Grace of Christ Revealed (1:16-17)
  c. Godhead in Christ Revealed (1:18)
 4. Priests (1:19-34)
  a. Interrogation of John by the Priests (1:19)
  b. Information about Christ from John (1:20-27)
  c. Identification of Christ by John in Public (1:28-34)
C. The Way (1:35-51)
 1. Concern Mutual in Finding Others (1:36,41,45)
 2. Contacts Made Personally (1:36,41,45)
 3. Conviction Manifest to Each in Turn (1:39,45,49)

II. RECORD OF LOVINGKINDNESS (2:1-12:50)
 A. John 2
  1. In Cana of Galilee (2:1-11)
   a. Sanctity of Marriage—He Was There in Presence (2:1-2)
   b. Sufficiency of the Master—He Was There in Power (2:3-4)
   c. Suggestion of the Mother—His Purpose for Being There (2:5-6)
   d. Surprise at the Miracle—He Performed There among Them (2:7-10)
   e. Sequel Manifested—His Personal Glory Revealed There (2:11)
  2. At Jerusalem (2:13-25)
   a. The Temple (2:13-17)
    (1) Conditions and Cleansing of the Temple Court (2:13-15)
    (2) Command of Christ regarding the House of God (2:16-17)

- b. The Traders (2:18-22)
    - (1) Challenge to Christ from His Enemies (2:18)
    - (2) Counter Challenge of Christ to Them (2:19)
    - (3) Claim of Christ and Its Confirmation (2:20-22)
- c. The Testimony (2:23-25)
    - (1) Passover—First during the Lord's Public Ministry (2:23)
    - (2) Publicity—Feast Day with Faith Following (2:23)
    - (3) Perception—Facts about All Are Known to Him (2:24-25)

B. John 3
  1. The Seeker (3:1-2)
     a. Coming to Christ—Determination Evident
     b. Connections to Consider—A Pharisee
     c. Confession to Christ—"Thou art a teacher"
  2. The Savior (3:3-5)
     a. Information about the Necessity of New Birth (3:3)
     b. Ignorance Revealed—No Understanding Shown (3:4)
     c. Insistence, There Is No Other Way (3:5)
  3. The Spirit (3:6-13)
     a. Manner of Spiritual Birth—Compared with the Flesh (3:6)
     b. Must of Spiritual Birth—A Call for Faith (3:7-8)
     c. Meaning Sought—Nicodemus Confuses the Facts (3:9-13)
  4. The Sign and Supply (3:14-17)
     a. Serpent Moses Elevated in the Desert to Save (3:14)
     b. Son of Man Elevated to Die to Save Sinners (3:14-15)
     c. Sacrifice Made Elevates the Dead in Sin to Salvation (3:16-17)
  5. The Sequel (3:18-21)
     a. Decision the Aim—"He that believeth on him" (3:18)
     b. Darkness to Avoid—"Men loved darkness rather than light" (3:19-20)

            c. Deeds to Attest—"That his deeds may be made manifest" (3:21)
        6. The Servant (3:22-36)
            a. Problem to Settle for John and the Jews (3:22-26)
            b. Pattern of Selflessness in John—"He must increase" (3:27-30)
            c. Personal Statement of John about Christ (3:31-35)
            d. Pardon for Sinners—Faith in the Person of Christ (3:36)
C. John 4
    1. Wayfarer and the Woman (4:1-9)
        a. Necessary Route to Find Someone Who Needed Him (4:1-5)
        b. Natural Rest—Being Weary He Sat at the Well (4:6)
        c. Need and Request—A Samaritan Woman with Problems (4:7)
        d. National Resentment—Segregation Practised (4:9)
    2. Well and the Water (4:10-15)
        a. Query—"If thou knewest"—She Did Not Know (4:10)
        b. Quality—"Living water"—A Gift from God (4:10)
        c. Questions—"Hast thou...?"—"Art thou...?" (4:11-12)
        d. Quantity—"Shall never thirst" again (4:13-14)
        e. Quest—"Give me this water" (4:15)
    3. Words and Worship (4:16-24)
        a. Command to Call and to Come with Her Husband (4:16)
        b. Chicanery to Cover the Questionable Associations (4:17)
        c. Comment to Clarify the Truth to This Woman (4:17-18)
        d. Contrast of Centers for Worship (4:22-24)
    4. Witness of the Woman (4:25-42)
        a. Woman and the Citizens of Sychar (4:25-29)
        b. Word of Christ to the Citizens (4:31-39, 41-42)
        c. Welcome to Christ to Stay in Sychar (4:40)
    5. Word that Works (4:43-54)
        a. Concern of a Father for His Son (4:45-47)
        b. Challenge of Faith for the Father (4:48)
        c. Cry of Fear by the Father (4:49)

            d. Course to Follow in Obedience to Faith (4:50)
            e. Cure, a Fact from the Moment of Obedience (4:51-52)
            f. Comfort of Faith Found in Testimony (4:53)
            g. Conviction of the Family (4:53)
    D. John 5
        1. The Sick Man (5:1-5)
            a. Circumstances at Bethesda—"The House of Mercy" (5:1-2)
            b. Crowd All Waiting Hopefully (5:3)
            c. Case in Question—One among Many (5:4-5)
                (1) Trial of Patience—Waiting Thirty-eight Years (5:5)
                (2) Test of Trying to Get There First (5:4)
                (3) Testimony of No Ability and No Assistance (5:7)
        2. The Savior (5:6-9)
            a. Compassion of Christ for This Man (5:6)
            b. Complaint in Contrast to the Question (5:6-7)
            c. Command of Christ to "Rise" and "Walk" as He Enabled (5:8)
                (1) Look
                (2) Rise
                (3) Take
                (4) Walk
            d. Cure Complete and Instantaneous (5:9)
        3. The Sequel (5:10-24)
            a. Enquiry of the Jews about the Lord (5:10-12)
            b. Exhortation of Christ to the Healed Man (5:13-14)
            c. Enemies of Christ on the Lookout for Him (5:15-16)
            d. Explanation of the Unity between the Father and Son (5:17-23)
            e. Evangel of Christ to Hearers and Believers (5:24)
        4. The Scriptures (5:25-47)
            a. Welfare of Believers Assured (5:25-29)
                (1) Anticipation of a Coming Hour of Blessing (5:25,28)
                (2) Authority of the Call Relating to Resurrection (5:25,28)

            (3) Answer to the Voice of Christ Asserted (5:25-29)
        b. Will of the Father Revealed in the Son (5:30-32)
            (1) "I Hear"
            (2) "I Judge"
            (3) "I Know"
        c. Witness of John the Baptist (5:33-35)
            (1) Bearing a Light
            (2) A Burning Light
            (3) Broadcasting Light
        d. Works of Christ a Witness for All to See (5:36)
        e. Witness of the Father in Christ (5:37-38)
            (1) They Heard Not
            (2) They Saw Not
            (3) They Received Not
            (4) They Believed Not
        f. Word of God for All Who Care about It (5:39)
            (1) Taste for Truth
            (2) Trust in Truth
            (3) Testimony of Truth
        g. Willfulness of Unbelief (5:40-47)
            (1) No Approach (5:40)
            (2) No Affection (5:42)
            (3) No Acceptance (5:43)
            (4) No Accusation from Christ (5:45)
            (5) No Agreement in Them (5:46-47)
E. John 6
    1. Question of Food (6:1-14)
        a. Need of the Multitude around the Lord (6:1-6)
        b. Nature of the Means Acquired by the Lord (6:7-9)
        c. Notoriety of the Miracle Accomplished by the Lord (6:10-14)
    2. Question of Fear (6:15-21)
        a. Alone—The Lord Absent from Them (6:15-16)
        b. Afraid—The Lake Agitated around Them (6:17-19)
        c. Assured—The Lord Able to Save Them (6:20-21)
    3. Question of Focus (6:22-71)
        a. Features Indicated by Christ (6:22-58)
            (1) Concerning Food (6:22-27)
            (2) Concerning Work (6:28-29)

John ◆ 65

                (3) Concerning Signs (6:30-40)
                (4) Concerning Complaints (6:41-51)
                (5) Concerning Strife (6:52-58)
            b. Facts Illuminated by Christ (6:59-66)
                (1) Baffled for Want of Spiritual Perception (6:59-61)
                (2) Benefits for the Believer in Christ (6:62-63)
                (3) Bankruptcy of the Flesh Offers No Profit (6:63)
                (4) Believing, the Foundation for Fellowship (6:64-65)
                (5) Backsliders Forfeit the Blessing (6:66)
            c. Fellowship in Identity with Christ (6:67-71)
                (1) Inquiry of Christ to His Disciples (6:67)
                (2) Identity Confessed by His Disciples (6:68-69)
                (3) Infamous Contrast in His Disciples (6:70-71)
    F. John 7
        1. Family Doubts (7:1-10)
            a. Familiarity Induced the Remarks to Christ (7:1-3)
            b. Feigned Interest Revealed Their Critical Minds (7:4-5)
            c. Forbearance Illustrated in the Restraint of Christ (7:6-10)
        2. Feasts Days (7:11-39)
            a. Ready to Listen to the Lord—A Mixed Reception (7:11-14)
            b. Reluctant to Learn—Too Many Side Issues (7:15,18,20)
            c. Recognizing the Lord (7:25-36)
                (1) Inquiry
                (2) Interest
                (3) Ignorance
        3. Facing Division (7:40-53)
            a. Discussion about Christ; For and Against (7:40-42)
            b. Division among the Crowd as a Result (7:43)
            c. Denouncements Aimed at Christ
                (1) Officers (7:47)
                (2) People (7:49)
                (3) Nicodemus (7:52)
    G. John 8
        1. Defendant (8:1-11)

                a. A Sinful Woman and the Religious Leaders (8:1-4)
                b. A Silent Woman and the Requirements of the Law (8:5)
                c. A Satisfied Woman and the Righteous Lord (8:6-11)
            2. Discourse (8:12-30)
                a. Light of the World is Christ (8:12-20)
                b. Lesson in the Words of Christ (8:21-25)
                c. Loyalty of the Son to the Father (8:26-30)
            3. Dispute (8:31-50)
                a. Ancestry Claimed from Abraham (8:30-40)
                b. Association Certified by Their Deeds (8:41-47)
                c. Accusation Cast at the Lord Himself (8:48-50)
            4. Derision (8:51-59)
                a. Deliverance Promised yet Misunderstood (8:51)
                b. Devil Possession a Taunt from His Enemies (8:52)
                c. Disbelief in His Person and Claims (8:53)
                d. Declaration Presented (8:54-58)
                    (1) Clarity
                    (2) Confession
                    (3) Claim
                e. Deadly Purpose Intended by His Enemies (8:59)
    H. John 9
        1. Circumstances of the Blind Man (9:1-7)
            a. The Man was Unable
            b. The Master was Undeterred
            c. The Method was Unique
        2. Command of Christ (9:7)
            a. Requirement—Obedience
            b. Response—Immediate
            c. Result—Satisfying
        3. Concern of Others (9:8-23)
            a. People (9:8-12)
            b. Pharisees (9:13-17)
            c. Parents (9:18-23)
        4. Courage of the Man Born Blind (9:24-34)
            a. Real Experience Had Taken Place (9:25)
            b. Recurring Enquiries from the Pharisees (9:26-27)
            c. Reply of Excellence to the Pharisees (9:28-33)
            d. Rejected and Expelled by the Pharisees (9:34)

5. Consolation for the Man Born Blind (9:35-38)
   a. Forsaken by Those Who Could Have Helped (9:35)
   b. Found by the One Who Could and Did Help (9:35)
   c. Faith in, and Fellowship with, the Son of God (9:36-38)
6. Condemnation (9:39-41)
   a. Sent to the Sightless—Seeing yet Sightless (9:39-40)
   b. Sin and Sight—Sight and Sin—in Contrast (9:41)

I. John 10
   1. Discourse on the Sheep (10:1-6)
      a. Contrast in Caring or Not Caring for the Sheep (10:1-2)
      b. Call to Be Heard and Followed as He Leads (10:3)
      c. Conduct of the Sheep with Shepherd or Stranger (10:4-5)
      d. Condition of Mind and Heart of the Hearers (10:6)
   2. Door of the Sheepfold (10:7-9)
      a. Person of Christ Himself the Door (10:7)
      b. Privilege of Entry—Salvation and Security (10:9)
      c. Perception in Recognizing the True from the False (10:8-9)
   3. Destroyers of the Sheep (10:10,12-13)
      a. Purpose of the Thief Clear (10:10)
      b. Principle of Personal Safety for the Hireling (10:12-13)
   4. Deeds of the Shepherd (10:10-11,14-18)
      a. Design to Give Life Abundantly (10:10)
      b. Decision to Die and Save the Sheep (10:11,15)
      c. Desire to Gather His Sheep into One Flock (10:16)
      d. Devotion to His Father's Will in This (10:17-18)
      e. Division among the Jews (10:19-21)
   5. Deity of the Shepherd (10:22-42)
      a. Request of the Jews for a Statement from Christ (10:22-24)
      b. Reiteration of Truth Already Expressed (cf. John 8:54) (10:25-30)
      c. Resentment of the Jews (10:31-33)
      d. Reasoning of Christ with Them (10:34-38)
      e. Retirement of Christ with His Disciples (10:39-42)

J. John 11
   1. Distress in a Home (11:1-16)
      a. Message of Martha and Mary to the Lord (11:1-3)
      b. Motive of the Delay in His Response (11:4-11)
      c. Meaning of the Delay Revealed by the Lord (11:12-17)
   2. Discussion (11:18-28)
      a. Comforters of the Family Were There (11:17-19)
      b. Confidence of Martha in the Power of the Lord (11:20-27)
      c. Claim of Christ Accepted by Martha (11:25-27)
      d. Call of Martha to Mary from Christ (11:28)
   3. Devotion (11:29-37)
      a. Devotion of Mary to Christ "at his feet" (cf. Luke 10:39; and John 12:3; 11:32) (11:29-32)
      b. Devotion of the Master to the Sisters (11:33-37)
   4. Demonstration (11:38-44)
      a. Labor of Moving the Stone, Theirs (11:38-41)
      b. Life-giving Voice of Almighty God, His (11:42-43)
      c. Liberty of Movement after Loosening the Grave Clothes (11:44)
   5. Delight and Dismay (11:45-48)
      a. Seeing and Believing the Mighty Work of Christ (11:45)
      b. Seeing and Betraying the Lord to His Enemies (11:46)
      c. Seeing and Bemoaning Their Own Impotence (11:47-48)
   6. Declaration of Caiaphas (11:49-53)
      a. Substitution—A Life for the Nation (11:49-50)
      b. Substitute—The Lamb of God Himself (cf. John 1:29) (11:51)
      c. Scope—Linking Together All in Himself (11:52)
      d. Scheme—To Bring about the Death of Christ (11:53)
   7. Discernment (11:54-57)
      a. Withdrawal from the Scenes of Dispute (11:54)
      b. Waiting for His Appearance among Them (11:55-56)
      c. Watching for His Appearance in Public (11:57)

K. John 12
　1. Supper at Bethany (12:1-11)
　　a. Occasion—Six Days before the Passover (12:1-2)
　　b. Offering of Ointment Sincere and Silent (12:3)
　　c. Odor Subjected All to its Influence (12:3)
　　d. Opportunist Wanted to Sell the Gift (12:4-6)
　　e. Observation—Her Service was Accepted and Appreciated (12:7-8)
　　f. Opportunity of Seeing and Believing (12:9-11)
　2. Spectacle (12:12-19)
　　a. Preparation for Christ's Entry into Jerusalem (12:12-13)
　　b. Presentation of Christ to the Nation (12:13-14)
　　c. Prophecy of Zechariah Fulfilled (cf. Zechariah 9:9) (12:14-16)
　　d. Petulance of the Pharisees Evident (12:17-19)
　3. Seekers (12:20-26)
　　a. Approach to Philip, Then Andrew, Then Christ (12:20-22)
　　b. Anxiety to See the Lord Expressed to Philip (12:21)
　　c. Answer Given by Christ to the Disciples (12:22-26)
　4. Sacrifice (12:27-41)
　　a. Purpose of the Hour: To Glorify the Father (12:27-28)
　　b. Power of the Person: To Draw All Men to Him (12:29-33)
　　c. Perception of the People: Deficient in Understanding (12:29-30, 34-36)
　　d. Proclamation of the Prophet Delivered to Them (cf. Isaiah 53:1,6,10) (12:37-40)
　5. Summary (12:42-50)
　　a. Fear and Reticence to Witness by Many (12:42-43)
　　b. Faith in, and Reception of His Word Alone Avails (12:44-47)
　　c. Facts for the Rejectors of His Word (12:48-50)

III. RELATIONSHIP AND LOYALTY (13:1–17:26)
　A. John 13
　　1. Passover of the Jews (13:1-17)

   a. Love of the Savior for His Disciples (13:1)
   b. Lowly Service of the Savior to His Disciples (13:2-12)
   c. Lesson Summarized for the Servants by Christ (13:13-17)
  2. Perfidy of Judas (13:18-30)
   a. News of Coming Treachery Disclosed (13:18-23)
   b. Name of the Betrayer Sought and Shown (13:24-29)
   c. Night of a Dark and Treacherous Deed (13:30)
  3. Precept of Jesus Christ (13:31-35)
   a. Concept of the Lord; Glory through Suffering (13:31-33)
   b. Commandment to Love Given to the Disciples (13:34)
   c. Continuation of Love Gives Proof of Discipleship (13:35)
  4. Profession of Peter (13:36-38)
   a. "Whither goest thou?" of Peter (13:36)
   b. Willingness of Peter to Follow the Lord (13:37)
   c. Weakness of Peter when Tested (13:38)
B. John 14
  1. Promise of His Return (14:1-6)
   a. Comfort through Faith in the Father and the Son (14:1)
   b. Confidence in Facts Now Revealed about Heaven (14:2)
   c. Condition Fulfilled in His Departure—A Threefold Promise (14:3)
   d. Concern about the Future and the Assurance of His Ability (14:4-6)
  2. Proof of a Relationship (14:7-11)
   a. Wish Expressed to See the Father (14:7-8)
   b. Witness and Expression of the Father in the Son (14:9)
   c. Words and Works of Christ Explain This Identity (14:10-11)
  3. Privilege and Responsibility (14:12-15)
   a. Promise to Answer Prayer in His Name (14:12-14)

              b. Purpose in Answering Prayer to Glorify the Father (14:13)
              c. Plea to Actively Practice on a Basis of Love for Him (14:15)
           4. Prayer for Residing Comforter (14:16-26)
              a. Indwelling of the Holy Spirit (14:16)
              b. Intentions Explained to Disciples by Christ (14:17-25)
              c. Instruction and Help Promised from the Spirit (14:26)
           5. Peace and Rejoicing (14:27-31)
              a. Personal Encouragement and Peace Given by Christ (14:27)
              b. Passing Events Provide Food for Thought (14:28-30)
              c. Purpose Explained "That the world may know" (14:31)
     C. John 15
        1. Fruit (15:1-6)
           a. Personalities (15:1-2)
              (1) Father
              (2) Son
              (3) Believers
           b. Purging Process and Its Purpose Stated (15:2-3)
           c. Progress Planned—Abiding, Then Bearing Fruit (15:4-5)
           d. Process of Parting the Bad from the Good (15:6)
        2. Fellowship (15:7-17)
           a. Foundation of the Fellowship—Abiding in Him (15:7-17)
           b. Fruitbearing That Follows—Love, Joy, etc. (15:7-17)
           c. Friendship and the Fidelity It Requires (15:14-17)
        3. Foes (15:18-25)
           a. Hatred for the Messengers of the Gospel (15:18-25)
           b. Hardness of Heart from Unbelievers Expected (15:18-20)
           c. Hostility a Foregone Conclusion (15:19-20)
        4. Fidelity (15:26-27)
           a. Spirit of Truth Sent from God—The Comforter (15:26)

        b. Spirit of Testimony as Seen and Heard of Him (15:27)
- D. John 16
  1. Persecution and Warning (16:1-6)
     a. Expressed by the Lord to Prepare the Disciples (16:1)
     b. Exclusion by the Leaders of the Religious World (16:2-3)
     c. Explanation by the Lord in View of His Departure (16:4-6)
  2. Person and Work of the Holy Spirit (16:7-15)
     a. Comforter, the Holy Spirit Promised (16:7)
     b. Conviction He Brings Affects All (16:8-11)
        (1) Conviction of Sin
        (2) Conviction of Righteousness
        (3) Conviction of Judgement
     c. Character of His Work to Glorify Christ (16:13-15)
        (1) Guide Us into Truth
        (2) Reveal Things to Come
  3. Preparation and Well-being (16:16-33)
     a. Departure and Return—A Question and Answer (16:16-33)
     b. Desire for Our Requests—The Scope in Prayer (16:23-24)
     c. Declaration and Revelation to the Disciples (16:25-33)
        (1) Plain Speaking to Them All (16:25-30)
        (2) Predicted Their Scattering (16:31-32)
        (3) Peace Secured for Them All (16:33)
- E. John 17
  1. Witness and Identity (17:1-5)
     a. Plea to Glorify the Son and the Father (17:1)
     b. Power to Give Eternal Life Theirs Alone (17:2-3)
     c. Pledge to Glorify the Father and to Be Glorified (17:4-5)
  2. Work and Interests (17:6-10)
     a. Statement "I have manifested thy name" (17:6)
     b. Summary of His Work to the Father (17:6)
        (1) "They have kept thy word" (17:6)

                (2) "They have known" (17:7)
                (3) "They have received...and believed" (17:8)
            c. Sequel—Personal Prayer for His Own (17:9-10)
        3. Wish and Intercession (17:11-26)
            a. To Keep Them, While in the World, from Evil (17:11,15)
            b. To Unify Them Wholly into One Flock (17:11,21-22)
            c. To Sanctify Them through the Truth (17:17,19)
            d. To Give Them His Joy (17:13)
            e. To Bring Them Home with Him in Glory (17:24-26)

IV. REJECTION OF THE LORD (18:1-19:42)
    A. John 18
        1. Pharisees (18:1-14)
            a. Infamy of Judas in Betraying the Lord, His Friend (18:1-3)
            b. Imposing Array of Guards to Take the Lord (18:3)
            c. Inquiry Involving Them All (18:4-9)
            d. Injury Inflicted on the Servant Malchus (18:10-11)
            e. Insult Inflicted on the Lord (18:12-14)
        2. Peter (18:15-18,25-27)
            a. Followed—Probably with the Crowd and John (18:15)
            b. Feared—Presuming He Was a Marked Man (18:16-18)
            c. Failed—Promised Fidelity Now Forgotten (18:25-27)
        3. Priests (18:19-24,28-31,40)
            a. Victim by His Own Will and Permission Alone (18:19-24)
            b. Vanity of Their Presumption and Pride (18:28-31)
            c. Verdict of Their Injustice with No Trial (18:40)
        4. Pilate (18:33-40)
            a. Interest in Christ as a Man (18:33-35)
            b. Indecision in Sidestepping the Issue (18:38-39)
            c. Injustice in Bowing to the Crowd (18:39-40)

- B. John 19
  1. Crucible of Suffering (19:1-15)
     a. Humiliation of Christ in the Hands of Sinners (19:1-3)
     b. Hostility and Cruelty in the Hands of Enemies (19:4-7)
     c. Hesitation, then Consent, by the Hand of Authority (19:8-15)
  2. Crucifixion of the Savior (19:16-37)
     a. Place—Golgotha, Place of a Skull (19:16-17)
     b. Placard with Its Announcement (19:18-22)
        (1) Publicity for All to See and Read
        (2) Provocation for the Priests
        (3) Plea of the Priests to Alter the Wording
     c. People Who Gathered to Watch Him There (19:21-25)
        (1) Some Hated Him
        (2) Some Loved Him
        (3) Some Were Indifferent about Him
     d. Presentation of Mary to John by the Lord (19:26-27)
     e. Passing and Dismissal of His Spirit (19:28-30)
     f. Prophecies of the Scripture Fulfilled (19:33-37)
        (1) Psalm 22:1-18
        (2) Psalm 34:20
        (3) Isaiah 53:3-9
        (4) Zechariah 12:10
  3. Care of Sincere Friends (19:34-42)
     a. Identity Made Public for All to See (19:38-39)
     b. Interest Personal and Real (19:38-40)
     c. Interment Prepared with Loving Care (19:40-42)

V. RESURRECTION OF THE LORD (20:1-31)
   A. Empty Tomb (20:1-10)
      1. Venture of Mary Magdalene to the Tomb (20:1)
      2. View of an Untenanted Tomb by Two Disciples (20:2-7)
      3. Verification of the Resurrection of Christ (20:6-8)
   B. Exalting Triumph (20:9-18)

       1. Over the Devil and His Designs
       2. Over Death and Its Despair
    C. Evident Truth (20:19-23)
       1. Person of Christ among Them Again (20:19)
       2. Proofs Conclusive—His Identity Established (20:20)
       3. Peace and Calm after the Storm of Doubts (20:20-23)
    D. Exception in Thomas (20:24-29)
       1. Doubts regarding Resurrection of the Lord (20:24-25)
       2. Delight Real in Seeing the Lord for Himself (20:26-29)
       3. Declaration and Response to the Lord's Presence (20:28)
    E. Enthralling Task (20:30-31)
       1. Record Incomplete yet Sufficient for the Need (20:30)
       2. Reason for Writing the Record—That We Might Believe (20:31)
       3. Resulting Faith Brings Life through His Name (20:31)

VI. RENEWAL IN LOVE (21:1-25)
    A. Frustrating Activity (21:1-3)
       1. Seven with Nothing to Do (21:1-2)
       2. Self-will Expressed for Old Ways (21:3)
       3. Sequel—Wasted Efforts in spite of Having Fished
          a. In the Right Place
          b. At the Right Time
    B. Fruitful Activity (21:4-8)
       1. Command of Christ (21:6)
       2. Catch from Christ (21:6)
       3. Conviction of Peter and the Others (21:7)
    C. Feeding Arrangements (21:9-14)
       1. Supply from the Lord Himself (21:9)
          a. Fire for Warmth
          b. Food for Hunger
          c. Fellowship to Meet Their Need
       2. Service Rendered to Them by the Lord Himself (21:12-13)
       3. Silence Reflecting on Their Present Experience (21:12)
    D. Focusing Affection (21:15-17)
       1. Three Denials of Peter in the Past
       2. Three Questions Asked of Peter in the Present

        3. Threefold Commission Given to Peter for the Future (21:15-17)
    E. Fitting Appointments (21:18-25)
        1. Declaration regarding Peter's Future (21:18-19)
        2. Desire of Peter regarding John's Future (21:20-21)
        3. Destiny of Each Disciple in His Hands (21:22-23)
        4. Disciples' Record concerning His Testimony (21:24-25)

Acts

Notes

1. This book was written about A.D. 63 by Luke, addressed to one named Theophilus, to whom he also addressed his Gospel (see Luke 1:3 and Acts 1:1).
2. The record covers more than thirty year's activity during which time the change from Judaism to Christianity was made.
3. It is a continuation of the Gospel story and sets forth the progress of the church of our Lord Jesus Christ.
4. Note the change from "they" in 16:8 to "we" 16:10, suggesting that Luke joined Paul in his missionary travels at Troas.
5. There are two major sections to this book; chapters 1-12 speak much of Peter and chapters 13-28 speak much of Paul.
6. Like Genesis, this book tells of the commencement of things, i.e. the first church, the first martyr, etc.
7. Three missionary journeys are spoken of here, referring to a large number of people and places.
8. A record of eight Pauline speeches is made in this book:
   1. At Antioch in Pisidia (13:16-41)
   2. At Lystra (14:15-17)
   3. At Athens (17:22-31)
   4. At Miletus (20:18-35)
   5. At Jerusalem (22:1-21)
   6. At Caesarea before Felix (24:10-21)
   7. At Caesarea before Agrippa (26:1-29)
   8. At Rome (28:17-20)
9. Luke was the only Gentile (non-Jew) to write a New Testament book. By vocation he was a physician.
10. Twice it is recorded that Paul spent two years in confinement (Acts 24:27 at Caesarea, Acts 28:30 at Rome).

GENERAL OUTLINE

I. WITNESSING IN THE NAME (1:1-7:60)
II. WITNESSING TO THE NEIGHBORS (8:1-12:25)
III. WITNESSING TO THE NATIONS (13:1-28:31)

DETAILED OUTLINE

I. WITNESSING IN THE NAME (1:1-7:60)
   A. Anticipating Pentecost (1:1-2:4)
      1. Introduction Given by Luke to Theophilus (1:1-2)
      2. Instructions Given by Christ to His Disciples (1:3-7)
      3. Intention to Give Power for Service to Disciples (1:8)
      4. Information Given by Heavenly Visitors (1:9-11)
      5. Interlude Giving Opportunity for United Prayer (1:12-14)
      6. Impulsive Choice by Vote in Anticipation of Repairing the Defection of Judas (cf. 9:15, God's Choice) (1:15-26)
      7. Indwelling Spirit of God in Power (2:1-4)
         a. Fellowship, "All with one accord" (2:1)
         b. Fire, "Cloven tongues" (2:3)
         c. Fulfillment, "They were all filled" (2:4)
   B. Action at Pentecost and Afterwards (2:5-7:60)
      1. Vocal Witness to a Mixed Company (2:5-47)
         a. Unity, "All filled...all these" (2:4,7)
         b. Uniqueness of the Situation, "All amazed" (2:7-36)
            (1) Charge and Answer Given by Peter (2:15-21)
            (2) Christ Crucified Acknowledged Publicly (2:22-35)
            (3) Clear Announcement concerning Him (2:36)
         c. Understanding of the Message, "When they heard" (2:37)
            (1) They Were Convicted
            (2) They Were Concerned
            (3) They Cried Out
         d. Urgency of the Counsel Given to Them (2:38-40)

e. Unhesitating in Their Reception and Continuation In (2:41-42)
     (1) Apostle's Doctrine
     (2) Breaking of Bread
     (3) Fellowship
     (4) Prayer
  f. Unquestionable Evidences That Followed (2:43-47)
     (1) Communal Possessions (2:43-45)
     (2) Continual Practice (2:46)
     (3) Contentedly Praising the Lord (2:47)
2. Vigorous Witness to All (3:1-4:37)
  a. Sufferer in the Temple Porch (3:1-8)
     (1) Helpless Man Carried There Daily (3:1-3)
     (2) Happy Miracle by the Name of Jesus Christ (3:4-8)
  b. Sensation It All Caused (3:9-11)
     (1) Recognized the Man That Was Healed (3:9-10)
     (2) Regarded the Miracle with Wonder (3:10)
     (3) Ran to Meet the Man and the Apostles (3:11)
  c. Sermon in the Porch (3:12-26)
     (1) Proclamation of Christ to the People (3:12-18)
     (2) Proposed Conversion by Repentance of the People (3:19-21)
     (3) Prophets and the Covenant Speak to Them All (3:22-26)
  d. Sanhedrin (4:1-3)
     (1) Arrest of the Two Apostles (4:1-3)
     (2) Addition of New Believers Recorded (4:4)
     (3) Answer of the Apostles to the Rulers (4:5-12)
     (4) Acknowledgment of the Counsellors (4:13-17)
     (5) Admonition to Desist Using the Name of Jesus (4:18)
     (6) Assurance of Faith Expressed by Peter and John (4:19-20)
     (7) Anxiety of the Counsel (4:21-22)
  e. Saints (4:23-31)
     (1) Report to the Company of Believers (4:23)
     (2) Resource in Confession and Prayer (4:24-30)
     (3) Renewal of Power by the Holy Spirit (4:31)

- f. Sales and Shares (4:32-37)
    - (1) Believers Sold Possessions (4:32)
    - (2) Blessing in Service Followed (4:33)
    - (3) Bounty Shared by All Who Had Need (4:34-35)
    - (4) Barnabas Sold Land and Surrendered All (4:36-37)
3. Violation in Witness (5:1-11)
    - a. Decision of Ananias and His Wife to Sell (5:1-2)
    - b. Deception Agreed in spite of Associations (5:2)
    - c. Devotion Acted by Them before the Apostles (5:2)
    - d. Danger Ahead Very Real in Lying to the Holy Spirit (5:3-4)
    - e. Death of Ananias on Hearing the Truth (4:4-5)
    - f. Dreadful Aftermath Inspiring All to Fear (5:6-11)
4. Victorious in Witnessing (5:12-42)
    - a. Authority of the Apostles Demonstrated in Power (5:12-16)
    - b. Animosity of Antagonists Revealed to All (5:17-18)
    - c. Angelic Ability to Deliver and Command (5:19-20)
    - d. Activity of the Apostles in the Temple as Result (5:21)
    - e. Anxiety of the Authorities Shown in Their Reactions (5:22-26)
    - f. Apostles Accused by the Rulers (5:27-28)
    - g. Apostles' Answer Clear and Unmistakable (5:29-32)
    - h. Astonishment and Anger of the Counsellors (5:33)
    - i. Advice Accepted by the Council from Gamaliel (5:34-40)
    - j. Affliction, Then Active Again in Teaching and Preaching (5:40-42)
5. Valor in Witnessing (6:1-7:60)
    - a. Decision and Choice regarding Deacons (6:1-8)
        - (1) Need for Men
        - (2) Number of Men
        - (3) Nature of the Men
    - b. Debate and Its Consequence, "Not able to resist" (6:9-10)
    - c. Destitute Characters Employed as Witnesses (6:11-14)

d. Disclosure to the Council, "His face as...an angel" (6:15)
   e. Discourse and Charge against the Council (7:1-53)
   f. Death and Cry of Stephen (7:54-60)
      (1) Sight of the Lord
      (2) Spirit Committed to the Lord
      (3) Supplication to the Lord

II. WITNESSING TO THE NEIGHBORS (8:1-12:25)
   A. Philip Preaching (8:4-40)
      1. Samaritans and the Power of God in Philip (8:4-8)
      2. Sorcerer Simon and His Out-of-focus Values (8:9-25)
      3. Seeker and the Sent One—Eunuch and Philip (8:26-38)
      4. Spirit and the Servant—Availability of Philip (8:39-40)
   B. Paul Planning (9:1-31)
      1. Concentration on the Work of Evil (9:1-2)
      2. Confrontation with Christ on the Damascus Road (9:3-6)
      3. Companions Hear a Voice but Do Not See (9:7)
      4. Conversion to and by Christ on the Way (9:6-17)
      5. Commitment to Christ for Service (9:18-20)
      6. Conflict in the Service of Christ (9:21-25)
      7. Courage in the Face of Opposition (9:23-26)
      8. Contact with Believers in Jerusalem Characterized by Fear and Friendship (9:26-31)
   C. Peter Proving (9:32-12:23)
      1. Miracles of Aeneas and Dorcas (9:32-43)
         a. Restoration of Aeneas from the Palsy
         b. Resurrection of Dorcas from the Dead
      2. Manifestation to Cornelius and Peter (10:1-16)
         a. Cornelius (10:1-8)
            (1) Angel
            (2) Actions
            (3) Assurance
         b. Peter (10:9-16)
            (1) Vessel
            (2) Variety
            (3) Voice
      3. Meaning of the Vision Shown to Peter (10:17-22)

4. Morrow a Venture of Faith for Peter (10:23-33)
5. Message of the Gospel Proclaimed to All (10:34-43)
6. Manner of Demonstration by the Holy Spirit (10:44-48)
7. Ministry of Peter Defended to the Jerusalem Elders (11:1-18)
   a. Contention of Some of Them (11:1-3)
   b. Case Explained to Them (11:4-14)
   c. Conversion of Those Involved (11:15-17)
   d. Contentment of the Believers (11:18)
8. Malice of Herod in Killing James, the Brother of John (12:1-4)
9. Ministry of Prayer Continued for Peter (12:5-11)
10. Mystery of Unbelief Even in Prayer (12:12-17)
11. Manner of the Man and His End—Herod (12:18-23)

III. WITNESSING TO THE NATIONS (11:1-28:31)
   A. Antioch (11:1-12:25)
      1. Formation of the Church at Antioch (11:19-21)
      2. Fellowship of the Church in Jerusalem (11:22)
      3. Fruitfulness and the Conditions Seen by Barnabas (11:23)
      4. Faithfulness of Competent Ministers (11:24-26)
         a. Integrity of Barnabas (11:24)
         b. Instructions of Barnabas and Saul (11:26)
         c. Identity of the Disciples with Christ (11:26)
      5. Feature of Real Conversion—Loving Gifts (11:27-12:25)
   B. Asia—First Missionary Journey (13:1-14:25)
      1. Selection of the Servants by the Holy Spirit (13:1-2)
      2. Separation by the Spirit for Their Special Work (13:2)
      3. Sending of the Servants by the Holy Spirit (13:2-4)
      4. Start of the Service in a Strange Land (13:5-14:25)
         a. Opposition at Paphos (13:5-12)
         b. Out-of-step at Perga (13:13)
         c. Opportunity at Pisidian Antioch (13:14-43)
         d. Opponents at Pisidian Antioch (13:44-52)
         e. Opposition at Iconium (14:1-7)
         f. Overcoming at Lystra (14:8-19)
            (1) Suffering Cripple Healed (14:8-10)

         (2) Surprise of the People (14:11-12)
         (3) Sacrificing Priest Appears (14:13-18)
         (4) Stoning of Paul by a Fickle Mob (14:19)
      g. Oppressed, Bruised, yet Onward (14:21-22)
      h. Organized Activity and Return to Home (14:23-26)
C. Antioch and Jerusalem (14:26-15:35)
   1. Laborers Report on the Work (14:26-28)
      a. Fulfillment
      b. Fellowship
      c. Fruitfulness
   2. Law and Its Relationship to Believers (15:1-5)
   3. Load of the Law Not for Believers (15:6-11)
   4. Liberty of the Believer in Christ Confirmed (15:12-22)
   5. Letter of Explanation Sent to Antioch (15:22-29)
   6. Loyalty of the Believers to the Word (15:30-35)
D. Asia and Achaia (15:36-21:17)
   1. Acts 15:36-16:40
      a. Contention between Barnabas and Paul over Mark (15:36-39)
      b. Companions Chosen by Each of Them for the Work (15:39-41)
      c. Consolidation of the Churches in Syria and Cilicia (15:41)
      d. Choice and Circumcision of Timothy at Lystra (16:1-3)
      e. Churches Confirmed As They Daily Increase (16:4-5)
      f. Control and Guidance Given by the Holy Spirit (16:6-8)
      g. Cry to Come Over and Help from Macedonia (16:9-11)
      h. Conduct and Communication at Philippi (16:12-15)
      i. Confession and Cure of a Demon-possessed Girl (16:16-18)
      j. Cause of the Complaint to the Magistrates (16:19-21)
      k. Confinement and Charge against the Apostles (16:22-24)
      l. Convulsions and Confusion at the Prison (16:25-26)

m. Conviction and Conversion of the Jailor (16:27-34)
n. Command for, and Circumstances of Their Release (16:35-40)
2. Acts 17:1-18:28
   a. Reasoning with the Jews in Thessalonica (17:1-3)
   b. Response to the Gospel by Jews and Greeks (17:4)
   c. Rioting by Unbelievers and Their Base Hirelings (17:5-9)
   d. Receiving and Reading the Word of God in Berea (17:10-13)
   e. Reflection and Resolve in Idolatrous Athens (17:14-17)
   f. Repentance the Remedy Even for the Religious (17:18-31)
   g. Resulting in Ridicule, and with Others Faith (17:32-34)
   h. Reasoning and Rejection of the Message (18:1-6)
   i. Residence of Paul for Eighteen Months in Corinth (18:7-11)
   j. Ruler Refuses to Intervene in a Dispute (18:12-17)
   k. Reason for Returning to Jerusalem and Antioch (18:18-22)
   l. Revisiting Assemblies in Asia with Untiring Zeal (18:23)
   m. Revelation of Scripture to Apollos (18:24-28)
3. Acts 19:1-21:17
   a. Uninformed about the Holy Spirit (19:1-7)
   b. Unbelief of Hardened Opponents to the Gospel (19:8-9)
   c. Unprecedented Publication of the Word and Demonstration of Power for Two Years at Ephesus (19:10-12)
   d. Uninitiated Sons of Sceva Pay the Penalty of Their Own Presumption (19:13-17)
   e. Uncompromising Break with the Past (19:18-20)
   f. Uproar over Idol Worship at Ephesus (19:23-41)
      (1) Cause
      (2) Character
      (3) Conclusion

            g. Unremitting Work of the Apostle and His
               Companions (20:1-16)
            h. Unceasing Watchfulness in the Care of the
               Churches (20:17-38)
               (1) Account of Service Given (20:17-27)
               (2) Anxiety Shown for Them All (20:28-31)
               (3) Affection Shared with Them (20:32-38)
            i. Undeviating Way Ahead for the Apostle Paul in
               spite of the Warnings of His Friends (21:1-17)
      E. Activity in Freedom (21:18-40)
         1. Report to the Elders at Jerusalem (21:18-20)
         2. Reason to Conciliate Jewish Believers (21:21-26)
         3. Riot to Incriminate Paul and His Friends (21:27-30)
         4. Rescue to Keep the Peace by the Romans (21:31-36)
         5. Request to Speak to the People Gathered (21:37-40)
      F. Arrested and Confined (22:1-24:27)
         1. Conversion and Conduct Recounted by Paul (22:1-21)
         2. Citizenship Claimed to Advantage by Paul (22:22-30)
         3. Confession to the Council in Jerusalem (23:1-5)
         4. Contention between Pharisees and Sadducees
            (23:6-10)
         5. Comfort for Paul from a Night Vision (23:11)
         6. Conspiracy to Do Away with Paul (23:11-15)
         7. Courage of Paul's Nephew in Speaking Up (23:16-22)
         8. Conducted to Caesarea under Escort (23:23-35)
      G. Anxiety of Felix (24:1-27)
         1. Indictment against Paul by Tertullus (24:1-9)
         2. Innocence of Paul Claimed before All (24:10-21)
         3. Indulgence of Felix toward Paul (24:22-23)
         4. Interest of Felix in Paul's Message (24:24-26)
         5. Injustice of Felix to an Innocent Man (24:27)
      H. Agrippa and Festus (25:1-26:32)
         1. Acts 25
            a. Animosity of the Jews after Two Years (25:1-6)
            b. Accusations of the Jews Unproven (25:7)
            c. Answer and Appeal of Paul to Festus and Caesar
               (25:8-12)
            d. Affair Explained to Agrippa by Festus (25:13-27)
         2. Acts 26
            a. Discourse of Paul—Record of His Service (26:1-23)

         (1) Politeness
         (2) Publicity
         (3) Promise
         (4) Persuasion
         (5) Power
         (6) Purpose
         (7) Performance
      b. Derision of Paul by Festus in Protest (26:24-25)
      c. Desire of Paul for Agrippa to Believe (26:26-29)
      d. Decision about Paul by Agrippa and Festus (26:30-32)
I. Assurance amid Fears (27:1-44)
   1. Forward to Rome—Not As Paul Would Have Chosen (27:1-3)
   2. Frustration and Ruin—Not As They Would Have Liked (27:4-20)
   3. Faith and Reassurance—Not of Their Own Making (27:21-25)
   4. Fasting and Rebuke—Not As the Sailors Wished (27:29-33)
   5. Food and Refuge—As God Promised His Servant (27:34-44)
J. Assistance and Friendship (28:1-22)
   1. Fire and Friendship Prepared and Offered to Them (28:1-10)
   2. Food and Fellowship Provided for Their Stay (28:1-10)
   3. Favors and Friends on the Way to Rome (28:10-17)
   4. Facts of, and Fidelity to, the Message Declared (28:18-22)
K. Announcement and Frustration of Paul (28:23-31)
   1. Design in the Declaration of Paul to the Jews (28:23)
   2. Decisions and Divisions That Followed Thereafter (28:24-25)
   3. Departure and Dullness of Heart Disclosed (28:25-29)
   4. Dedication under Duress by Paul—Witnessing for Two Years While under House Arrest (28:30-31)